Your husband drives so fast that it scares you. Your family won't share the housework. Your mother is full of put-downs. Your co-workers smoke and you can't stand it. Your boss gives you work so late in the day that you miss your ride home.

In situations like these, women's rights come off the speaker's platform, where they have been fought out in recent years. Now these issues are waiting for solutions on your own home grounds, where *Effectiveness Training for Women (E.T.W.)* deals with them in a down-to-earth, everyday way for the first time.

E.T.W. is an entirely new program. It is not the assertiveness training you've heard about. Step by step, with many case examples and actual dialogues, it demonstrates precisely *how* you can overcome traditional female passivity and dependence; how you can master fears of self-disclosure, confrontation, conflict. You can stop worrying that you're "unfeminine" when you speak up for your rights. And you can quit spending too much of your time living for others.

E.T.W. gives you much more. It shows you specific new skills so you can overcome the personal problems that society has inflicted on women, and shows how to

(continued on back flap)

Ethel K. Smith Library

**Wingate University
Wingate, North Carolina 28174**

Effectiveness Training
for Women
E.T.W.

Effectiveness Training for Women E.T.W.

Linda Adams with Elinor Lenz
Introduction by Dr. Thomas Gordon

WYDEN BOOKS

Manufactured in the United States of America.

First Edition

Trade distribution by Simon and Schuster
A Division of Gulf + Western Corporation
New York, New York 10020

Library of Congress Cataloging in Publication Data
Adams, Linda.
    Effectiveness training for women, E.T.W.
    Includes bibliographies and index.
    1. Women—Psychology. 2. Assertiveness (Psychology)
3. Sex role. 4. Interpersonal relations. I. Lenz,
Elinor, joint author. II. Title.
HQ1206.A23   301.41'2   79-12277
ISBN 0-87223-553-X

Contents

To my parents, Dorothy and Robert Williamson
To my husband, Tom, and
To my daughter, Michele

Introduction

THIS BOOK HAS a history in which I have been involved in very personal and meaningful ways. The fact that Linda Adams happens to be my wife has forced me to experience for the first time what it's like to live with someone glued to a desk chair in our study for months, sweating out a publisher's deadline. From this reversal of roles in our relationship I have acquired much more understanding of what she so often has endured in the past.

Even more meaningful is how my personal and professional relationship with Linda has contributed to raising my consciousness about women and the unique problems they experience in relationships.

My professional focus had always been on training people who possess the *most* power in relationships, beginning with my Parent Effectiveness Training (P.E.T.) program and continuing with the development of effectiveness-training courses for teachers (T.E.T.) and for leaders (L.E.T.). It had not occurred to me to design a training program for women, who in many of their relationships possess the *least* power. Now I consider it fortunate that Linda, fresh from having earned her Master's degree in Sociology with a major in Women's Studies, opened my eyes to the need for a training program uniquely designed to teach women the skills for personal effectiveness in their relationships—particularly with male friends and husbands, with coworkers and bosses, with friends and associates of the same sex.

During the period in which she was designing Effectiveness Training for Women, with the help of Tony Zener of our staff, my understanding of the status of

women in our society expanded and deepened considera-
bly. I came to understand how little girls are programmed
at home and at school to be unassertive and not self-
disclosing; how girls are subtly influenced to take on roles
in which they are expected to be sacrificing and nurturant
for others; how men consciously and unconsciously
(through their behavior and language) reinforce this sex-
role stereotyping.

My learning was not all that intellectual or academic.
My wife's direct and open self-disclosures continually exposed my own sexism, as well as the inequities I fostered
in relationships with women. I became aware of how ludi-
crous it was to call grown women in my organization
"girls"; how degrading it was to the women who felt I
treated them too often as sex objects; how inequitable it
was for me to make decisions about *our* money without
consulting my wife; how indefensible was my initial resistance to Linda's decision to keep her name after we married.

These were not the only insights resulting from having
the woman's course designed within my organization and
this book written under the roof of our house. I have come
to understand much better the tragic consequences of my
own mother's giving over control of her life to my father
—how her growing dependency led to a period of depression and paralyzing loss of self-esteem. And it became
much clearer how my first wife's alcoholism served as an
escape from her unwillingness to look for personal
achievement and self-esteem outside our marital relationship.

My education did not stop there. I have also come to
appreciate more fully how essential it is for women to be
effective in getting their needs met in their relationships
with their husbands if they are ever to use the parenting
skills taught in P.E.T. An unfulfilled, unhappy, needful
wife will not muster much motivation (or even intent) to

stop and listen empathically and acceptingly to her child's problems. Nor will she want to foster a reciprocal (democratic) relationship with her children if she is denied such a relationship with her husband.

It is my present conviction that many mothers who overlook or ignore their needs for satisfying relationships outside the home, and/or needs for achievement and accomplishment in meaningful work, make themselves vulnerable to disappointment and disillusionment when they discover, sometimes too late, that motherhood by itself has failed to bring them satisfaction of all of their needs.

As a result of all of these learnings, I changed—from thinking that an effectiveness-training course for women would be a good idea to feeling very strongly that it is an important program. And this growing excitement about the course more recently has been strongly reinforced by the evidence we get of its strong impact, particularly from participants' written evaluations, some of which you'll read in this book.

Many women, housewives and employed persons alike, will find that the skills taught in Effectiveness Training for Women and described in detail in this book will make it easier for them to identify unmet needs and make plans to get them met; build reciprocal relationships in which mutual need satisfaction can become the norm; and resolve conflicts with people without power, without winners and losers.

When more women are able to make these things happen in their lives, we are certain to see some fundamental changes in our society and its institutions. After all, women make up more than half of that society. Effective women can do much to bring about a more effective society.

Thomas Gordon
Founder, Effectiveness Training

1. BECOMING A MORE EFFECTIVE PERSON

*If I am not for myself, who will
be for me? If I am for myself only,
what am I? If not now—when?*

BABYLONIAN TALMUD

In the early years of this century, whether you looked back to the past or ahead to the future, you would have had difficulty seeing yourself as a unique and separate person. Your life probably would not have been very different from your mother's or your grandmother's, and you would have expected your daughter's life to follow the same general pattern as your own. The limited choices open to women made it almost inevitable that their lives would have a predictable quality. Regardless of differences in ability, interests, or aspirations, most women would move along a prescribed path from childhood to old age.

Here and there, an exceptional woman—a Margaret Mead or Eve Curie—would strike out boldly in directions considered highly atypical for her sex. But for the most part, women lived much as they had always lived—defined by their relation to others. Many of us still do.

Seeing yourself primarily in relation to others makes it very difficult to develop a firm sense of your own identity, or to think seriously about (and develop yourself into) the kind of person you would like to be.

Today, because of changes in our society, we have been learning what we want *freedom from*—from having our

1

lives controlled by others, from being so dependent on others, from being treated as second-class citizens politically and socially, from limited aspirations, from rigid sex-role stereotypes.

Now, a new kind of freedom is opening up to us, *freedom to* shape our own lives and make ourselves into the kind of people we want to be. Now the choice can be ours. That can be exhilarating, but also frightening. The frightening aspect obviously is linked to the risk that always exists when we must decide among alternatives and take responsibility for our decisions. But this very process of choosing and taking control will keep us in touch with ourselves and give us a unique identity. This is how we take responsibility for our lives and achieve the goals that are important to us.

The purpose of this book is to provide a philosophy and a set of skills to help women achieve this goal while maintaining balanced and satisfying relationships with others. Through step-by-step instructions, you will learn that:

You can take control of your own life.

You can act to meet your needs while still respecting the needs of others.

You can prevent some problems and conflicts through self-disclosure.

You can confront others effectively and sensitively when their behavior interferes with your meeting your needs.

You can deal with your anxiety about being more open and direct.

You can resolve conflicts without damaging relationships.

You can deal effectively with value conflicts.

You can listen effectively when another person has a problem.

You can set goals and make plans to achieve them.

Taking control of your life and assuming more responsibility for meeting your needs is an essential first step—especially for women who have spent most of their time and energy concentrating on the needs of others.

Chapter II will describe some ways you can gain more control over your own life—by becoming more aware of your needs and wants and by deciding to exercise your freedom to carefully consider, select, and put into action decisions that will help you get your personal needs met.

Having determined your needs, wants, values, and goals, you can start moving toward meeting them. This is a large part of what it means to control your life, and yet it is often a difficult transition for the woman whose sense of self has been grounded in her identity as a wife and mother. Having viewed herself primarily as someone expected to serve the needs of others, she is uncertain and confused about meeting her own needs. She may even feel guilty about separating her needs and drives from those of her family. "It seems egotistical and unfeminine" is a common reaction of women when they first consider becoming self-directing and taking control of their lives.

One of the skills taught in E.T.W. for increasing one's sense of internal control and responsibility is self-disclosure (or assertiveness).* Self-disclosure means clear, honest, authentic communication about oneself, while at the same time preserving respect for the other person.

Taking more control of your life does not mean isolating yourself or putting distance between yourself and others. All of us, to a greater or lesser extent, are dependent on our relationships with others as a source of meeting our needs—for love, companionship, fun, sexual gratification, support, and many other things.

In later chapters, you will see how many benefits can accrue to all your relationships from open, honest, and direct self-disclosure of your opinions, beliefs, and per-

*The terms "self-disclosure" and "assertiveness" will be used interchangeably throughout this book.

sonal values. And we'll explain how you can do this without putting others down.

Another important result of exploring your needs and wants is that you will realize how much of your *time* is spent in meeting others' needs. While living cooperatively is clearly desirable, sometimes what we do for others gets out of balance with what we do for ourselves. If you often find it hard to say "no" when people ask you to do things you really don't want to do, you'll want to start using the Responsive I-Message, a communication skill for making clear to others that their request is not acceptable to you.

To prevent some of the unpleasant and often unnecessary conflicts with people in your life, we offer the Preventive I-Message to help you communicate your future needs, especially when what you want or need will affect others. As a part of each I-Message we stress the importance of changing your posture from disclosing to listening when others indicate their discomfort with what you say.

Further, in all your relationships with others—children, spouses, friends, parents, coworkers, supervisors—it is inevitable that, in the pursuit of getting their needs met, their behavior will at times interfere with some legitimate need of your own. For example, the way your husband drives scares you; your mother always puts you down with her criticism; one of your coworkers is a week late with a report you need; your boss has been making a habit of giving you work so late in the day that you miss your bus home.

What do you do at such times? Keep your negative feelings to yourself and feel resentful? Tell them how thoughtless and inconsiderate they're acting? Neither choice is very effective. However, there is an alternative approach. You can take the initiative to confront the other person about unacceptable behavior in such a sensitive way that you don't damage your relationship. In Chapter VII this method will be fully explained and illustrated. It's called a Confrontive I-Message—a stronger form of self-disclosure.

The thought of being self-disclosing often brings on a great deal of anxiety. Do I have a right to stand up for my needs? How will others react? Will they dislike me? Will they get defensive? Will they think I'm selfish? How to handle anxiety associated with honest self-disclosure will be dealt with in a subsequent chapter.

Conflict is an inevitable consequence of living and working with people. They want one thing, you want another. There is a clash of wills. Who is to win? If you win at the other's expense, she or he will feel resentful and angry. If you lose and the other person wins, *you're* going to feel resentful or angry. In either case, the relationship may suffer. In Chapter X we'll describe the No-lose Method of resolving interpersonal conflicts, a six-step problem-solving process that leads to solutions acceptable to both parties—no one feels either a winner or a loser. Consequently, there is less resentment, fewer power struggles, and higher motivation for each to carry out the solution.

The chapter on values collisions can help you identify and understand how critical they are. You'll learn some ways of resolving values-related problems and some effective ways of trying to influence others to change their values.

In Chapter XIII a definite shift occurs from dealing with the skills of solving problems that *you* own—that is, where you take an active role in confronting others, get them involved with you in conflict resolution, or act as a helpful consultant. In all your human relationships you will also encounter situations with other persons who are troubled, hurting, frustrated, upset, depressed—quite independently of you. *They* have a problem in their own lives. To have mutually satisfying relationships, everyone must be willing to lend an ear, to act as listener or counselor, to help others find solutions to *their* problems. Yet often, instead of listening, we impose our advice or solutions; we preach and moralize; we interrupt the flow of communication with questions, evaluations, or reassurances.

We will describe and illustrate ways you can become a more effective "helping agent" to the people in your life. With practice, you'll find these skills can really work, provided you're feeling good enough about yourself to give your time and attention when others are not feeling so good about themselves.

Finally, in Chapter XIV, we offer some ideas and methods that can help you make specific plans for achieving your goals. Because your planning and goal-setting will work better if you sort out your goals by categories and learn a method of precise planning to help you accomplish them, we offer a systematic approach so you can separate short-term from long-term goals, and a six-step process by which you plan to achieve them.

Becoming more effective in your personal life and in your interpersonal relationships naturally doesn't happen overnight, and no one ever arrives at some final destination—becoming a totally effective person. Achieving competence in personal problem-solving and goal-setting as well as in the skills of building and maintaining satisfying and rewarding relationships is always a process—and a never-ending one.

One E.T.W. graduate describes her own process this way:

"The course made me more aware of *myself*—and the way I react to various situations in my everyday life. I'm more aware of my needs and how important it is for me to express how I think and feel to other people. In turn, I feel better about myself and am more satisfied. I guess I expected I'd change drastically through the course, but it's hard to develop new patterns of relating to other people and a new way of thinking, and I realize it takes time to change. To learn the E.T.W. skills, they must be practiced and used. I have a long way to go, but E.T.W. has given me enlightenment and skills and a better understanding of myself."

II. GAINING MORE CONTROL OF YOUR LIFE

To know oneself is the first of duties.

LA FONTAINE, *Fables*

A basic concept of E.T.W. is the idea of control of one's own life. Although the word "control" has many negative connotations, and often conjures up the image of one person controlling the behavior of another, we are defining "control" in quite a different way. In this context it means that you can be an active agent in meeting your own needs; you can make decisions and take actions to meet your goals, particularly at those times when what you want does not depend on the cooperation or participation of other people.

YOUR "AREA OF FREEDOM" TO CONTROL YOUR LIFE

Obviously, you do not and cannot have *total* control of all your life. Your personal area of freedom is that part of your life in which you are free to make independent, unilateral decisions about issues in your life that do not depend on the cooperation or participation of another person. You have the freedom to consider, select, and implement solutions to meet your own personal needs. Your area of freedom might include:

1. Changing your beliefs about a certain issue

2. Learning a new skill

3. Getting more time to relax, have fun

4. Deciding whether, how much, and what you want to read, music you want to hear

5. Looking for a better job

6. Joining a particular religious group or political party

7. Choosing what kind of physical exercise you want

8. Deciding what doctor (and other experts) you want to consult

In many other instances not only are you dependent to some extent on the cooperation of others, but they are also affected by the decision. Therefore, you do not normally have as much freedom to make independent decisions. In these cases, other people would probably be involved with you in the consideration, selection, and implementation of decisions. Some of these situations might be:

1. Quitting your job

2. Changing your family's vacation plans

3. Rearranging the office you share with a coworker

4. Having a party in your home

5. Investing your family savings in real estate

6. Deciding to move your family to another city

7. Increasing your salary

8. Adopting a child

The essential difference between these two categories is the area of freedom that exists for you. Obviously, the items in each list will vary from one person to the next, and from one relationship to another. You probably have a different area of freedom in each of your relationships

—with your spouse, your children, your parents, your friends, your boss. You might have a very large area of freedom in your relationship with your spouse, and a much smaller area of freedom in your relationship with your boss, or vice versa. And if you live alone you obviously have a much greater area of freedom than if you live with other people.

We can think of decisions that might ideally belong on the first list but are treated by many women as if they were on the second—joining a political party, for example, or taking a particular course at a university. Often the reluctance to take a controversial position for fear of producing a conflict, or to spend on themselves time that they feel should be devoted to others, has prompted women to place limitations on making such decisions.

So while we recognize the many realistic limits that keep us from having total control of our own lives, many of us can assume much more personal responsibility for getting more of our own needs met.

What we are trying to counter is an attitude in many people that they have no control over what happens to them. While many people in our society feel a lack of "fate control," this is particularly common among women—and for a variety of reasons. Generally speaking, women have been taught to be dependent on others—parents, husbands, even children. We have been taught not to take responsibility for meeting our own needs. We have been socialized to believe that we will receive our greatest satisfaction and fulfillment in meeting the needs of others—our children, spouses, bosses, parents. In this role it is necessary to be *responsive* to others' needs rather than *initiating* actions that could meet our own needs.

No wonder that so many women find themselves feeling they have no control over their own lives.

As more and more of us realize that just responding to

others' needs is not enough to satisfy our own needs for personal achievement, we are beginning to take more responsibility for ourselves. One of the main purposes of this book is to provide a stronger base for the value of assuming more personal responsibility, and to provide some skills that can help women meet some of their important needs.

BENEFITS OF GETTING MORE CONTROL OF YOUR LIFE

It requires courage to take more responsibility for getting your own needs met, because while many of us know the security of allowing others to take responsibility for meeting many of our needs and make decisions for us, we don't know the benefits of our taking responsibility for our own lives.

In addition to the obvious benefits of getting more of your needs met, you enjoy many other significant advantages, some of which are:

As you gain more courage and confidence to act in your own behalf, your self-worth will increase, and will continue increasing with each new situation.

You will begin trusting your own perceptions more; you will have less need for others to agree with you.

You will become less dependent on others for your sense of self-worth, because you will be getting it from your own achievements. You will become less dependent on others' positive judgment of you.

You will have fewer feelings of anger, anxiety, and depression, because you are successful in disclosing yourself in more real and spontaneous ways.

You will feel less hostile and resentful as more of your important needs are satisfied.

Your relationships with others will be better—more effective, more satisfying. As you experience yourself as a responsible, initiating, acting person, your life will become more satisfying.

These benefits are illustrated by reports from women who took the E.T.W. course:

"I feel that I now have choices for what I want to do with my life and that these choices are entirely up to me. I can hold no one else responsible or ask anyone to make my decisions for me, which is something I have done for a long time. I still have a very long way to go, but for the first time in my life I feel there might be a light at the end of the tunnel."

"Before E.T.W. I felt like a doormat. Now, with the skills I have learned, I no longer have that feeling. I now realize that what I have thought and kept to myself all along *is* important. I have the right to express my needs and to be respected for it. I also have learned that even though others have needs and must be respected for those needs as well, I have the right *NOT* just to step aside and let them have their way. That there is a way so that both can feel they have 'won.' I really feel a lot better about *me* as a person. I have learned to really like myself because now I don't find myself thinking, 'Why didn't I say something when I had the chance?' Now I have the skills and plan to use them the rest of my life."

"I have a new feeling of confidence, of control over my behaviors. Many of them arose from fears about imposing my feelings on others. E.T.W. has given me a tremendous feeling of personal power in terms of how I cope, but more important, how I interact with my environment. For years I have been extremely polite and self-effacing with my peers, to my own disadvantage. *Passive?* Not any more I'm not!"

"The course has helped me to identify my style of life, i.e., letting situations control me more than I would like. It has shown me that *I* can and do control my own life and must take charge of my own situation by the hour, day, year. It has taught me many ways to do these things—some new; others that were familiar were made clear."

Deciding to take personal responsibility often requires changes in attitudes. While it can be an exciting, challenging process, it can also be frightening. You realize that you alone are ultimately responsible for your actions and decisions—that you must depend on yourself for knowing and satisfying many of your important needs.

Perhaps an enlightening way to look at it is to remember that you have always had control. So far you have chosen to exercise it in a certain way; now you are going to make some different choices.

WHO CONTROLS YOUR LIFE?

To evaluate the degree of control you have over some major parts of your own life, think about the following questions in terms of *how much control you actually take* (not how much you wish you would take).

Your Body

Is your body important to you?

How much control do you have over it?

Control over how it looks?

Control over what you eat?

Control over how it functions?

Control over how much exercise you get?

Control over what doctor tends to it?

Control over how much rest you get?

Do you want to take more responsibility for your body?

If so, how could you do so?

Your Money

Is money (and what it can provide) important to you?

How much control do you have over money in your life?

Control over whether or not you earn money?

Control over how much you earn?

Control over how money gets spent?

If you want to take more responsibility for money and its use in your life, how could you go about it?

Your Work

Is work important to you?

How much control do you have over the work you do (inside and outside your home)?

Control over what type of work you do?

Control over how much or how hard you work?

Control over where you work?

How could you take more responsibility for work and its place in your life?

Your Time

Is your time really valuable to you?

How much control do you have over how you spend it?

Control of the "free time" you have?

Control of whom you spend time with?

Control of time you have alone?

Does the way you spend your time satisfy you?

How might you assume more responsibility for the way you spend time?

Your Life

Is your life really important to you?

How much control do you have over getting what you really want out of life?

Control over the way you're living it at present?

Control over who is part of it?

Control over future plans and goals?

Control over where your life is spent?

How might you take more control of your own life?

If you take less control in any of these areas than you would like, ask yourself what keeps you from assuming more control. Can you change that? If not, why not? If so, how?

GAINING MORE CONTROL REQUIRES AWARENESS OF YOUR NEEDS AND WANTS

Getting some awareness of your personal needs and wants is a first step in taking more responsibility for your life. Although the idea of knowing one's own needs and wants seems obvious, it is not at all—especially for women who have been trained to think of others' needs, to be nurturant, giving unselfishly to children, family, bosses. A woman may have been in the position of meeting the needs of others for so long that it's difficult, perhaps even impossible, for her to think positively of her own needs. Women tell us:

"I have always tried to please my husband and children. I never thought too much about myself."

"I was taught to believe that spending time on myself and doing what I wanted to do was selfish—and I feel guilty when I do it."

For many women, a major step is the realization that they have the *right* to meet their important needs. This and the subsequent step of becoming more aware of what some of their important needs are often require the peeling back of layer after layer of socially imposed demands and expectations. This is challenging, rewarding, and an essential first step in becoming more effective.

In the E.T.W. course women start by inspecting their lives in specific ways: how they spend time, what they value, like, and dislike, and what changes they would like to make.

Becoming more aware of how you actually spend your time day by day and how you feel about it can give you an indication of which present needs of yours are being met, and which ones are not. We suggest that you keep a log for several days noting precisely how you spend all of your time. For example:

7:00 A.M.   Got up, took shower, got dressed, made bed

7:30   Made coffee, fed dog and took dog out, made breakfast

7:45   Ate breakfast, read newspaper

8:15   Cleared breakfast dishes, cleaned up kitchen, got food out for dinner

8:30   Dropped daughter at school, mailed letters, put gas in the car, went to 9:00 meeting . . .

This exercise can provide you with valuable insights about how you actually spend time and help you recognize that you have some needs that you may not have been thinking about or acting on. It is the first step in your being able to make changes so you can meet more of your important needs.

This process of thinking about your needs and the changes you would like to make takes various amounts of time and energy, depending on how much such self-searching you have done before and how deeply you want to engage in it now. You may come up with needs that involve only slight changes in your life, or with very important needs that can affect your relationships with others.

The kinds and levels of needs you have and the types and degrees of changes you want to make are matters of personal choice. We are not advocating any particular needs or wants you *should* or *should not* have. We are suggesting a *process* by which you can become more effective in meeting your own personal needs. These needs can be of many kinds: emotional, psychological, material, physical, recreational. They can include a need or want to:

Have more free time

Get married

Get a college degree

Get a better job

Get divorced

Learn a new skill

Become more athletic

Be with your children more often

Get a job to earn money

Get a job for personal achievement

Not have children

Get involved with an interesting group

Have a baby

Travel

Have more friends

Improve your relationship with your parents

Whatever your own personal needs include, this is merely a first step in a series of moves that, hopefully, never ends. As you gain confidence in your ability to meet more of your needs, on your own and in your relationships with others, you will become involved in new challenges, new situations, new problems, and will continue to analyze, assess, and evaluate your needs.

For example, at one point in your life you may have strong needs to have children and spend a good deal of time with them; at another point you may have strong needs to achieve some professional goals. Or, as is becoming more and more common, you may find it necessary to work to earn money. Then you can set out to find and get prepared for jobs you would like to have in the future.

When you have some idea about the needs in your life

that you want to meet, the next step is learning ways to bring about changes in your life in an effective way, especially when those changes will affect other people. As we have said, one of the basic ways to meet personal needs, and bring about changes, is through self-disclosure.

III. SELF-DISCLOSURE: HOW TO DO IT EFFECTIVELY

Through spontaneity we are reformed into ourselves. Freed
from handed-down frames of reference, spontaneity
becomes the moment of personal freedom when we are
faced with a reality, explore it, and act accordingly. It is
the time of discovery, of experiencing, of creative
expression.

VIOLA SPOLIN

THE courage and ability to translate feelings and thoughts into language so others can know you and you can know yourself is a powerful, exciting way of communicating. Much of the E.T.W. course (and this book) is based on the value of self-disclosure and its importance in helping you get more of your important needs met. Before discussing the benefits and risks, let's consider the ways we usually communicate with others about our important needs.

Don't we customarily communicate openly and honestly with others—unless we are intentionally and deliberately trying to deceive them? In fact, clear and honest communication with others is unusual for most of us. We tend to communicate with each other through our roles rather than our true selves. We are trained throughout our lives to hide our true selves— our thoughts, feelings, and opinions. From our earliest years, the message is drummed into us that there are acceptable and unacceptable ways of representing ourselves to others, and that we should adapt ourselves to the acceptable ways. Slowly but surely, we build up a façade of securities and defenses behind which we present ourselves to others in ways that have very little to do with who we really are.

As we adapt to what we have been taught is acceptable, we take on styles of communicating that can be roughly classified as nonassertive or aggressive. While only a few people are either completely nonassertive or aggressive, many more of us alternate between the two. Some of us tend to be nonassertive until we get very resentful because we have so many unmet needs; then we become very aggressive. And some of us act aggressively until we feel so guilty that we get nonassertive. Both postures have some advantages, but both have serious disadvantages, which become evident as we describe them.

WHAT IT MEANS TO BE NONASSERTIVE

Nonassertive behavior means not expressing your feelings, thoughts, needs, wants, opinions to others—failing to act in self-directed ways to meet your important needs.

Nonassertive people make a conscious effort to avoid conflict, even when it means they will suffer. They react rather than act; they spend much time and energy responding to what others say and do, instead of taking the initiative for communicating and acting on their own. They often subordinate their needs to those of others. So people take advantage of them—for example, by making decisions for them, ignoring their inputs, or giving them more work.

Fear is a major contributing factor to much nonassertive behavior:

Fear of losing in a conflict; need to save face

Fear of getting disapproval or disagreement from others; need to be liked and accepted at all costs

Fear of being rejected or ignored or finding that others don't care what you think or need

Fear of losing control—i.e., losing your temper, exploding

Fear of hurting or rejecting others

Many nonassertive people are so overcome with anxiety that they won't express even their most ordinary feelings, needs, and opinions. When they do express their ideas or needs, they often do it in such a self-effacing way that other people disregard or ignore them. Nonassertive people are therefore often angry, frustrated, and resentful, and spend much time and energy later wishing they had said or done something that would have made others aware of them.

How do you know when you're behaving in a nonassertive way? If you're not getting your important needs met, not feeling satisfied, not achieving your goals, it *may* be due to nonassertive behavior. Your most reliable indicators are your feelings of continuing anxiety, dissatisfaction, resentment, or anger, especially after an interaction with someone.

Here are some examples:

You would like very much to be involved in making up your family budget this year, something you haven't done in the past. You don't mention your need to your husband. When you notice him working on the budget, you start feeling upset and anxious.

In your job, you have worked very hard during the past year and have instituted several new procedures to help your department operate more efficiently. Although you would like to get a raise (and feel you deserve one), you don't mention this to your boss. You keep hoping he'll bring it up. He doesn't—and you find yourself becoming frustrated and unmotivated.

Such nonassertive behavior is most common among people in subordinate positions who have been discouraged from assuming control and responsibility for themselves. It is characteristic of many women, because they so often have been rewarded for being agreeable, polite, and cooperative.

WHAT IT MEANS TO BE AGGRESSIVE

Aggressive behavior means getting one's needs met but doing so at the expense of others; being insensitive or outright antagonistic to others' feelings, ideas, and needs. Aggressive people, unlike their nonassertive counterparts, openly express their feelings, opinions, and needs, but in ways that humiliate, disregard, or hurt others. In extreme aggressiveness, relationships are strained or destroyed, which is why aggressive people find it increasingly difficult to meet their needs when the cooperation of others is necessary. Another kind of aggressive behavior, not so blatant or visible but much more common, is passive aggression, or getting one's needs met through manipulating others, deceiving them, sabotaging their efforts to meet their needs, or stubbornly and silently resisting them.

Your internal indicators of aggressive behavior are feelings of guilt or embarrassment. More important, you get negative reactions from others—they may avoid you, act resentful and angry toward you, isolate you, or retaliate by behaving aggressively toward you.

If you want to participate in the budget you might tell your husband:

"I demand to have a say in our budget—I'm tired of being left out!"

If you want a raise, you say to your boss:

"If I don't get a raise, I'm going to look for another job."

WHAT IT MEANS TO BE ASSERTIVE

Assertive behavior means knowing what you need and want, making this clear to others, working in a self-directed way to get your needs met while showing respect for others.

Above all, being assertive requires honest self-disclosure. Assertive people communicate honestly and directly; they express feelings, needs, and ideas and stand up for their rights, but do so in ways that don't violate the rights and needs of others. They are authentic, congruent, open, and direct. They are capable of acting in their own behalf; they take the initiative in meeting their needs. They ask for information and for the assistance of others when they need it.

When they have a conflict with others, they are willing to work for solutions that satisfy both parties. Since assertive people often need and want cooperation from others in meeting their needs, they're willing to cooperate and help when others are trying to meet their needs.

You will know you are behaving assertively when you experience feelings of reduced anxiety and increased satisfaction, self-esteem, and self-confidence; and when more of your important needs are being met. Also, others will often respond more positively to you, and some of your relationships will become more satisfying.

You would be assertive if you said to your husband:

"I'd like to be involved in making up our budget this year. I'd like to learn more about it—and also there are some things I need that I hope can be included."

If you said to your boss:

"I'd like very much to discuss getting a raise in my salary—I feel I've improved our department a lot this year."

BENEFITS OF EFFECTIVE SELF-DISCLOSURE

The most important benefit of disclosing yourself to others is that it enables you to keep in close touch with yourself—your needs, your opinions, your ideas. Communicating an idea to others is an entirely different process from merely thinking about the idea. The act of saying something aloud transforms it. You've probably had the experience of mulling a particular problem over and over in your mind so much that it got bigger and bigger and seemed much worse. You imagined outcomes and conjured up others' reactions. Later, when you did relate your problem to someone else, it came out in an entirely different way.

Through the experience of self-disclosure to others you get to know yourself intimately. Then you can act more concretely on how you feel, and through that process you create more opportunities to develop yourself in new and exciting ways. It can become an exciting cycle of growth and change.

A related benefit of your continual self-disclosure is that you live in the present. When you can stay constantly in close touch with yourself, you can meet your present, current needs.

Failure to communicate spontaneously causes you to live in the past or in the future, struggling internally with how to deal with your troubling thoughts, feelings, and needs.

Further, self-disclosure makes it much more possible for you to get your important needs met when help or cooperation from others is necessary. When other people know what you need and want, they are more able and willing to cooperate with you to help you meet some needs. We often make the mistake of assuming that other people know us so well that they know how we feel, or what we want; we shouldn't have to tell them. Failure to tell others about our needs in close relationships can have lasting negative effects:

"I shouldn't have to tell him how I feel—if he really cared about me, he'd know."

"We've lived together for twenty-five years and she knew how much this meant to me, and she didn't change. Now it's too late —I don't care anymore."

The willingness to express needs and desires to others brings about such effects as these reported by E.T.W. participants:

"My husband is more aware of my needs and more interested in helping me meet those needs. He is also more able to assess his own needs—there were things he wanted to do himself but wouldn't do."

"People I've felt free to share my feelings with have actually seemed to care."

"My husband has accepted me more as a person in my own right."

"Because my boss now realizes how pressured I am in the outer office, he is careful to prioritize things he wants me to do and seems to plan ahead a little better so I don't have too many rush jobs."

"My family now knows I have definite needs and they're willing to listen and sometimes even willing to help me achieve satisfaction of my needs."

"My boyfriend appreciates me more now that I'm able to say what I feel instead of always agreeing."

Self-disclosure makes you a more interesting person, too. The cover-ups and pretenses people design for themselves are rarely as interesting as their authentic selves. When we fail to disclose our distinctive needs, attitudes, and opinions, we deny our individuality. Our encounters become dull and superficial. The excitement of our thoughts and experiences is filtered out.

Another very important benefit of being self-disclosing is your increasing self-esteem. It's incredible how much better you can feel about yourself when you have the courage to be open and honest with others, especially about ideas and issues that are very important to you. Your self-esteem and confidence can continue to increase, because self-disclosure becomes easier to do each time you succeed, as these women in E.T.W. classes report:

"As I begin to think more highly of myself, people are beginning to accept my ideas, share, and care—and it makes everyone feel good."

"It seems like people are more comfortable with me because I'm much more open with them about how I feel about things. It was always easier *not* to be assertive—to be passive and passive aggressive. Now that I'm aware of my feelings I'm happier with myself and more comfortable with others."

"Now when I talk to my husband I'm not afraid to say what I feel. He listens to me and then we discuss it."

"I feel like now I am a real person."

"I like myself better."

"I have more self-confidence that I can carry out a plan."

There is a lot of evidence that self-disclosure is reciprocal. Because your willingness to be self-disclosing opens the way for others to be self-disclosing too, many of your relationships are deepened and enriched. Many misunderstandings can be cleared up and future ones avoided. Frustrations and resentments decrease. As you discover mutual interests, as well as others that are new to you, your range of friendships and activities can expand. As others become more self-disclosing and get in closer touch with themselves, they can begin to take more responsibility for their own lives and for meeting their important needs. Women in E.T.W. classes reported these outcomes of their self-disclosures:

"As I learned to 'unmask' and be myself when communicating with others, they naturally responded with true gut-level communication."

"My relationships with certain people close to me have improved since I've been more able to express my feelings and have encouraged them to do the same with me."

"In the case of my children, I have let them know my needs and opened the door for better communication. They in turn began to do the same."

"My husband expresses his feelings more now instead of keeping them inside."

Self-disclosure can keep relationships from becoming damaged. As we all know, incongruent communication often causes the breakdown of relationships, and has been a major factor in many divorces.

A woman who is a successful writer tells of how she learned, after having an abortion, that although her husband said he supported her decision, he actually was unable to express his true feelings. When he finally did, he told her that he had really wanted another child. The marriage subsequently broke up. "We were having other problems," she explains, "but I think the abortion and my husband's inability to express his true feelings about it were among the crises that precipitated our separation."

Women report these benefits of becoming more self-disclosing:

"My husband and I relate *much, much* better."

"I find I have more honest relationships with a few people, especially some I was in conflict with before."

"My husband and I communicate more."

RISKS OF SELF-DISCLOSURE

Self-disclosure can bring disagreements and conflicts to the surface. These are often disagreements that you have avoided in the past by not talking about them. When you get the courage to state what you believe or how you feel about particular issues, you leave little room for doubt. Others may then disapprove of you, even reject you. They may argue or fight with you. Although bringing such disagreements and conflicts out in the open can be a very positive outcome of self-disclosure, in some cases relationships can suffer, as illustrated here:

"I am having more conflict with others at this time. So many people expect me to serve them and I haven't been. I notice definite confusion from people around me. I am determined my life is going to change. I feel a confidence in me that my needs and values have a right to be recognized also."

"Every time I get the courage to express my opinion about women's rights, my boyfriend starts a big argument about it and tells me how wrong I am."

"My husband has been revealing things I say or do to him that hurt him. It hurts me at the time, but I know him better this way."

"I am no longer a rubber stamp as before. Not everyone enjoys this."

There is a risk, then, that some of your relationships may change or end. Your willingness and courage to be self-disclosing, especially where you have been nonassertive in the past, may cause changes that you have not expected or are not prepared to handle.

Often, self-disclosure is the moment of truth in relationships, especially if there has been little honest interaction. When one person finally gets the courage to express her or his honest feelings, all the pretenses of the past are shattered and the relationship can't survive.

"I thought of Chris as one of my close friends, but recently we've been having some pretty honest and deep discussions, and I'm finding we really don't have much in common after all."

"My husband I never talked about our problems. When he decided to leave, he told me all the things he didn't like about me—when it was too late for me to do anything about it."

Quite obviously, before you consider sharing your feelings and needs with others, you must have trust in them. You are not likely to disclose yourself to people you think might laugh, criticize, ignore, or repeat what you tell them about yourself. But when you trust someone, you are relying on that person's commitment to the relationship. As your trust is reinforced, the relationship continues to grow.

THE SKILL OF SELF-DISCLOSURE: I-MESSAGES

In the E.T.W. course, self-disclosure takes the form of I-Messages. An I-Message is a statement that describes you; it is an expression of *your* feelings and experience. It is authentic, honest, and congruent. And since I-Messages express only your inner reality, they do not contain evaluations, judgments, or interpretations of others.

Since you are saying what you really feel, your verbal and nonverbal (body language) expressions are in harmony. Your messages come through confidently and congruently. You avoid the possibility of confusion in the other person. In most cases, this inspires respect, acceptance, and cooperation from others. They perceive you—and you perceive yourself—as responsible, independent, resourceful, and in control of your life.

In E.T.W. we teach four different kinds of I-Messages:

Declarative I-Messages*

Responsive I-Messages

Preventive I-Messages

Confrontive I-Messages

Since each kind of I-Message has a somewhat different purpose, we have arranged them in a hierarchy according to the level of risk and difficulty usually associated with each one. In this chapter we will describe the most basic and least risky one—the Declarative I-Message.

---

*In the E.T.W. course we have called this a Disclosing I-Message. Because that seemed redundant, we changed the name to Declarative I-Message.

DECLARATIVE I-MESSAGES

Declarative I-Messages are your self-disclosures to others about your beliefs, ideas, likes, dislikes, feelings, reactions, interests, attitudes, and intentions. They let others know what you are experiencing, what it feels like to be you. They describe your inner reality.

Since Declarative I-Messages allow others to know you better and to understand more about you, it's possible for them to relate with you more honestly. These messages also invite and encourage others to share their experiences with you, so you can form more meaningful relationships.

Every day you probably share much about yourself in this way with people with whom you have close relationships:

"I sure am excited today."

"I feel a little sad right now."

"I really don't like movies with a lot of violence."

"I like the way our staff meeting went today."

"I enjoy playing tennis."

"I'm tired."

"I don't like talking on the phone."

"I value time with my family."

"I enjoy discussing controversial issues."

"I feel rushed this afternoon."

"I love you."

"I dislike flying."

"I appreciate your help."

Since Declarative I-Messages are expressions of your personal perceptions and opinions unrelated to others, they do not generally cause others to react in defensive or resistant ways. Nevertheless, you will want to be prepared to handle any resistance constructively, should you encounter it.

RESISTANCE TO I-MESSAGES

A common response to your I-Messages will be acceptance, agreement, understanding, and even excitement (especially after others get accustomed to your assertiveness), but at times you can expect others to feel upset or defensive. This is more likely if a lot is at stake. As we said before, Declarative I-Messages generally entail the least risk of resistance or causing people to become threatened. As you progress to the more difficult and risky kinds of I-Messages (Responsive, Preventive, and Confrontive), resistance from others is much more frequent.

Defensiveness or resistance indicates the other person's discomfort with your I-Message. It is a natural, inevitable response when someone feels threatened. Sometimes your I-Messages can surprise, shock, or catch others off guard. I-Messages may produce anger, anxiety, fear, and hurt in others, and cause them to react (at least initially) in a defensive or resistant way.

How Do You Know When the Other Is Resisting Your I-Message?

When you send an I-Message, you almost always get some kind of response from the other person. Some obvious verbal and nonverbal clues that indicate resistance are:

Verbal	*Nonverbal*
Yelling	Getting silent
Arguing	Looking sad or hurt
Making sarcastic remarks	Crying
Joking	Looking surprised or shocked
Changing the subject	Laughing
Refusing to talk about it	Looking away
Disagreeing with you	Leaving the room
	Pouting

Here are some typical dialogues:

You: I liked the way our staff meeting went today.

Coworker: Boy—I didn't! I felt frustrated and angry the whole time!

You: I enjoy our discussing controversial issues.

Husband: Well, I don't—you always have to be right!

You: I believe a woman should have the right to get an abortion if she wants to.

Friend: I can't believe you said that! Abortion is the same as murder.

When an I-Message causes such reactions from others, they need to vent their feelings before they're going to be able or willing to hear what you want to say.

SHIFTING GEARS—FROM DISCLOSING TO LISTENING TO DISCLOSING

When you express your needs and opinions in I-Messages and do get resistance, you will almost always defeat your purpose if you continue to repeat your self-disclosure. Reasserting your need or opinion in the face of resistance usually comes across as aggressive and insensitive. It puts others even more on the defensive and stiffens their negative reactions to what you are trying to communicate. What they hear from you is: "This is what I want [or think], regardless of how you feel about it."

To increase the chances that the other person will hear your I-Message, you need to listen and acknowledge her or his upset feelings. A willingness to be sensitive to the other's feelings and concerns is what separates assertive from aggressive behavior. Even though you send a very clear I-Message, if you fail to take into account the other's negative feelings, you are in effect saying: "I want to be heard or get my needs met no matter what!"

Therefore, as soon as you become aware of the other's resistance, you should "shift gears." After sending your I-Message you shift to listening to the other's feelings; from initiating to responding. You now want to be sensitive to the other's feelings. You want to show concern for —and a genuine desire to understand the needs of—the other person. She or he now hears an attitude like this from you: "Here's what I value. But I'm willing to stop and listen to you, because I value you and respect how *you* feel."

This temporary shift to the other person's concern sets up a conciliatory atmosphere. It communicates your sensitivity to (and interest in) her or him. It lets others know you're not out to get your needs met at their expense. Shifting gears does *not* mean you abandon your needs or your convictions. It does mean you recognize that dealing with the other's resistance is an integral and indispensable step in getting your own needs met, that you value the other person and are interested in her or his feelings too.

One shifting of gears (to listening) is often sufficient to help the other person vent her or his negative feelings. At other times you may find it necessary to shift back and forth from disclosing to listening several times.

Your willingness to listen effectively also provides an opportunity for both of you to clarify your intentions and needs. And, if necessary, it prepares the way for problem-solving.

Your willingness and ability to listen in a sensitive and respectful way is often sufficient to lower resistance, so when you return to your original assertive message, it has a better chance of being heard and accepted. Acceptance does not mean agreement, but rather a willingness to tolerate a different point of view or a new situation.

When you shift gears from disclosing to listening, you maintain a balance between your concern for yourself and your concern for others—a key to effective communication and reciprocal relationships.

ACTIVE LISTENING TO RESISTANCE

Active Listening is a special way of reflecting back what the other person has said, to let her or him know that you're listening, and to check your understanding of what she or he means.

It's a restatement of the other person's *total* communication: the *words* of the message plus the accompanying *feelings.* To shift gears to Active Listening, you must temporarily put yourself in the other's position, try to get a sense of the other's thoughts and feelings, and then share your understanding with the other to check its accuracy.

This Active Listening sequence consists of these steps:

1. You receive the other's "coded" message, verbal and nonverbal.

2. You "decode" the message and get your sense of what the other is trying to communicate.

3. You feed back your understanding of the other's message, saying in effect: "Here's my understanding of what you're feeling or experiencing. Am I right?"

4. The other person then reacts to your Active Listening response, confirming or clarifying your understanding of her or his message.

Let's take the example in which you said to your husband: "I enjoy our discussing controversial issues."

Husband   You

Your husband puts his feelings into a verbal message (we call it encoding) and says:

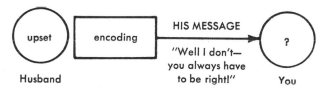

You then try to understand (decode) the message, to get a sense of what he is communicating.

You then feed back your understanding of his message, saying in effect: "Here's my understanding of what you're feeling. Am I right?"

HIS MESSAGE

upset — encoding — "Well I don't— you always have to be right!" — decoding — he sounds upset

Husband

You

"You're upset by the way
I behave when we talk about
things like that."
YOUR ACTIVE LISTENING RESPONSE

Then you can expect your husband to respond to your Active Listening response, confirming your understanding of his message: "That's right" or "You got it."

Whether you Active Listen again or continue self-disclosing depends on how strongly he feels. Your continued sensitivity will help you determine that.

You can see how this works when we apply it to another situation. Suppose that a dialogue with your friend about her report to the neighborhood association goes like this:

You: I think you did a good job on the report, but I disagree that this neighborhood should be rezoned for apartments. It'd change the character of the neighborhood and spoil it for the homeowners. (I-MESSAGE)

Friend: That's a pretty rigid point of view. I'm really surprised to hear you say that! (RESISTANCE)

You: I see you're upset about what I said. I'm interested in knowing more about why you feel the way you do. (SHIFTING GEARS TO ACTIVE LISTENING)

Friend: I believe apartments would attract more single and elderly people and I think that would be really good for the neighborhood. We need more variety.

You: This is important to you: living with people of different ages and lifestyles. (ACTIVE LISTENING)

Friend: Yeah, and one reason it's important is because I'd like my children to have exposure to different kinds of people.

You: You think they'd benefit from knowing lots of different people. (ACTIVE LISTENING)

Friend: I really do. I think we could have homeownership along with apartments and it would improve the neighborhood.

You: You really believe we could have the best of both worlds. (ACTIVE LISTENING)

Friend: Yeah—that's right.

You: I sure see your point. But what I love about this neighborhood is how quiet and peaceful it is. I guess I'm afraid that would change. (ANOTHER I-MESSAGE)

By shifting gears, your discussion has opened up to accommodate a basic values difference on this issue.

Let's look at the situation in which you and your friend clash on the emotional issue of whether a woman should have the right to get an abortion. You may be tempted to reassert:

"I do mean it, and I don't see why you're so upset about it."

Instead, you shift gears to Active Listening:

You: What I said really upsets you. You must feel very deeply about this. . . .

Friend: I certainly do! I was brought up to believe that life is sacred and must be protected at all costs.

You: So the idea of abortion offends one of your most important beliefs—

Friend: Yes—and besides that I think it's being taken too lightly these days.

You: You mean that too many women are getting abortions maybe without thinking about other choices. . . .

Friend: Yeah . . . I just think there are better ways to handle it than to end a life. . . .

You shift gears again, this time returning to your assertive message:

You: Yeah—I agree with that part. But I do think that abortion is better than having a baby that isn't wanted. . . .

Again, a potentially inflammatory encounter has been cooled down, and without either party backing away from her own feeling. A basis has been established for rational dialogue on this and other controversial issues that might come up.

Active Listening is helpful even when it's somewhat off target, because it helps the sender think about the thoughts or feelings she or he has just expressed. Even if the Active Listening feedback is not quite accurate, the sender has a chance to correct it by sending another message. If the Active Listening response is accurate, then the asserting person can continue her communication.

When the other person feels she's been heard, she is much more likely to listen to your opinion or need when you restate it.

After Active Listening to resistance, you often come to understand the other person better or find out something you weren't aware of. New information may prompt you to modify your original I-Message to some extent. It may also make clear the existence of a conflict between the two of you that cannot be solved through self-disclosure and listening. (We'll discuss how to resolve such conflicts in a later chapter.)

For many people, Active Listening seems unnatural, phony, and mechanistic when they first try it. Since it's a different way of responding from what we're used to, Active Listening is a difficult skill to learn. However, when your attitude toward what the other person feels is one of acceptance, that will come through—and Active Listening will become more natural.

To summarize: remember that your success in getting others to hear you (and thereby help get your needs met) depends not only on your ability to express yourself in honest, clear ways but also on your willingness and ability to listen and allow others an opportunity to express themselves.

In this chapter we've described Active Listening as an effective way of reducing the other's resistance, and thereby helping you meet your own needs. Chapter XIII will demonstrate the use of Active Listening in an entirely different context: how you can learn to be an effective "helping agent" when another person has a problem.

IV. LEARNING TO SAY "NO"

Genuine responsibility exists only where there is real responding.

MARTIN BUBER

WHEN you have explored your needs, wants, and values and have begun to develop a clearer sense of direction, you will find yourself becoming more aware of how much time and energy you spend on activities that don't meet your personal needs. Many women report their surprise at this discovery:

"I've been letting situations control me all my life without realizing I could change them."

"My time and energy are constantly being exploited by others."

"I've always had this unsatisfied feeling at the end of each day about all the things I wanted to do and never did."

After analyzing how you actually spend your time, you'll discover the proportion of every day that you give over to the needs and wants of others, with much of that activity having no relation to your own needs and wants. For some women, this proportion runs as high as 80 percent, and some are shocked to discover that it's 100 percent!

Why do we permit our lives to be taken over this way? Why do we so often say "yes" when we want to say "no"? An immediate answer suggests itself: saying "yes" is easier and more pleasant; it's hard and often painful to say "no." Let's examine this further and see *why* it's so difficult, particularly for women.

Throughout human experience, people have struggled with trying to meet personal needs as well as community needs. Each of us is a person with an inner life that is unique and special; at the same time, each is one of the parts that add up to (and fit in with) a whole—the society or social system in which we live. Obviously, if we're living within a system and deriving benefits from it, we owe that system something—but how much? And how do we reconcile conflicts between the system's needs and our own?

As we challenge traditional roles and pressures to conform, these questions take on a new urgency. For centuries, women's roles have been largely predetermined and their choices limited. Our individual needs have often been judged secondary to those of social groups: the family, church, community. So we have often responded with an unconditional "yes" to the demands of these social institutions. We have been so imbued with this principle of service and duty to others that we frequently lose track of our obligations and responsibilities to ourselves.

Today, women have more options. And if we want to take control of our lives and become fully dimensional and assertive human beings, we need to assess more carefully this problem of saying "yes" when we mean "no." Unless we can understand our motivations, chances are we will continue to let our concern for others outweigh our concern for self.

WHY WE SAY "YES"

When someone asks you to do something you would rather not do, you may feel a strong impulse to say "no," but then frequently find that the impulse will be accompanied by anxiety. You may feel under pressure to comply, to demonstrate you're agreeable, pleasant, cooperative. Saying "no" sets off negative feelings, and many are rooted in our upbringing. Somewhere deep within us is that "good little girl" who always went along with what was expected of her. Otherwise, she was tagged as "selfish" and disloyal, and she was warned: "People won't like you."

Many forces are at work to make us feel that the price of saying "no," real or imagined, is too high. Here are some reasons why we say "yes" when we'd rather say "no":

REASONS	EXAMPLES
Surprise	"Well, okay . . . I guess I could do it." "I haven't thought about tomorrow, but I guess I could."
Desire to please, need for approval	"I want her to like me." "I'd like to make them happy."
Fear of hurting others	"She'd be so hurt if I said no." "I'm afraid I'll hurt his feelings if I don't go."
Fear of punishment or loss	"He'll never forgive me." "They'll never invite us to anything again."
Guilt	"How could I go on living with myself?" "I'd feel so selfish."
Deference to authority	"They know more about these things than I do." "I have to do it, she's my boss."
Reciprocation	"I may need the same sometime." "One good turn deserves another."

Conformity to cultural expectations	"I believe in being cooperative." "What will the others think?"
Identification	"What if I were in her shoes?" "I know the feeling all too well."
Duty or sense of obligation	"It's my duty as a citizen." "I owe it to my family."
Martyrdom	"I'll suffer through it." "I'll manage somehow."
Need for power	"It'll give me a chance to get in with some VIP's." "If I refuse they'll think I'm not up to it."

The element of surprise is a major factor in saying "yes" when you would rather say "no" and when you're uncertain what you want to do. Because you're unprepared or unsure, you say "yes" without really considering your needs. Often this can cause you to get resentful and angry, and to have negative feelings about the other person. Consider the following typical requests:

"Would you baby-sit for me this afternoon?"

"Can we drop by for a few minutes this evening?"

"Could you feed our dog while we're away this weekend?"

"Can we borrow your movie camera to take on our vacation?"

Just because someone has requested something of you doesn't mean you must respond immediately and positively. Instead of automatically saying "yes" (or "no," for that matter), more congruent responses might be:

"I need to think about it. Let me call you back in a few minutes."

"I'd like to discuss it with the rest of the family. I'll let you know as soon as I can."

This can give you time to think and decide without feeling so much pressure to comply. Then, when you decide to honor (or not) the other's request, you know you've done so in a responsible, self-directed way; you can feel good about your decision and about the other person.

Some of the other reasons why we say "yes" to requests —not wanting to hurt others, duty, reciprocation, identification—can work positively for us as individuals or as members of society. Other times, they tend to push us into a nonassertive position so we lose initiative and sense of personal control. It's legitimate to want to be perceived as a "good" person, someone who cares about others, someone willing to lend assistance. And if your concern for others is genuine, it can be a strong motivation to respond to the requests and demands that come your way. But remember that you also have a right to look after your own needs, to make choices and decisions that bring meaning and satisfaction to your life. What you want to consider most is achieving a comfortable *balance* between independence and interdependence. You can ask yourself:

How can I organize my life to fulfill my needs and attain my goals?

How much time, energy, and resources do I need to commit to meeting my needs and attaining my goals?

What am I willing to do for others?

What am I presently doing for others?

How much of my time, energy, and resources am I willing to commit to the needs of others?

Do I want to do more for others?

Each of us will find different answers. Your own proba- bly will vary at different stages of your life. When your children are growing up, you may be more willing to comply with requests from the school, the PTA, the Scouts, or similar organizations. At other stages, you may be more interested in lending support to cultural and educational activities, or civic causes. The important thing is to find the balance that works for *you*—really feels consistent with your particular needs—at any given time.

SAYING "NO" WITH RESPONSIVE I-MESSAGES

The communication skill we teach in E.T.W. for responding to unacceptable requests from others is the Responsive I-Message—a message that clearly communi- cates "no" when "no" expresses your authentic feelings. Two parts make up a good Responsive I-Message: (1) your self-disclosing message (or assertion) and (2) how the re- quest will affect you.

1. Your Self-Disclosure (Assertion)

This part of the I-Message clearly expresses your deci- sion to decline the request. It can take several forms:

"No, I don't want to."

"I have decided not to."

"I'm choosing not to."

These statements have a crucial element in common—they accurately communicate your conscious choice, your decision.

Although each person will find her own style and tone, it's important to avoid such statements as:

"I can't."

"I won't be able to."

"I'm too busy right now."

Such statements convey that you're not in control of your life, that you're not responsible for your decisions or actions. Your "no" sounds as if it's not your own autonomous decision, as if it's being imposed on you by external forces. It therefore sounds tentative and unreliable. It invites people to argue with you. While you may be feeling strongly unaccepting, your incongruent message communicates a measure of acceptance. Not so the Responsive I-Message.

"I choose not to" leaves no doubt that you're the source of the decision. The disowning response "I just can't" invites the reply "Why not?" When you say "I'm too busy right now," you may imply that you could do it later. It leaves you open to "How about some other time?" Now you have a dilemma: do you comply with the new unacceptable request, or do you continue to disown responsibility by falling back on additional excuses or lies?

2. The Request's Unacceptable Effect on You

The second part of your Responsive I-Message tells why you choose to say "no." It's not always necessary to provide reasons to support every decision to decline a request. Saying "no" in a responsible way sometimes is sufficient, especially if you don't know the other person very well. Just being able to say "I've decided not to go," without giving any reasons or explanations, is in itself a benefit experienced by many women in the E.T.W. course.

However, in most cases it's advisable to support your decision with your reasons, so the other person doesn't get the impression you're being rude, arbitrary, or aggressive, and understands you're consciously choosing to meet some other legitimate needs. You are, in effect, communicating:

"I am choosing not to honor your request, but I value our relationship, and trust you'll respect my reasons for my decision."

Expressing the reasons for your decisions also helps you clarify and affirm your decision, which reinforces your self-awareness.

The unacceptable effects of a request may come as a tangible or intangible consequence that you anticipate, should you agree to carry out the request. Suppose someone asks you to devote substantial time to some project or activity that is of little or no interest to you. The tangible consequences might include: loss of money, loss of time for other activities, negative effect on health, on family or some other relationship. The intangible effects on you might include: worry, pressure, boredom. All of these possible consequences, tangible and intangible, would enter into your decision to say "no." Your Responsive I-Message might be: "No, I've decided not to work on the committee this year, because I've done it for five years now and I'm tired."

Here are Responsive I-Messages you can use in reply to unacceptable requests:

"No, I really don't want to lend money right now; I need it for some things in my life."

"No, I'm choosing not to attend any meetings for a while, because I have a really important project I want to give all my attention to."

"No, we don't want to buy any magazines, because we already subscribe to more than we have time to read."

"No, I've decided not to go shopping with you next week; I'd like to spend some time with my family."

"No, I don't want to go out to lunch today; I am trying to diet and I get too tempted when I'm in a restaurant."

"No, I don't want to buy any copperware, because it costs more than I want to pay."

"No, I don't want to come to a Tupperware party, because I already have a lot of it I don't use because it can't be put in the dishwasher."

Very often, such clear, congruent messages are met with understanding, acceptance, even relief. Many people will respect you more for being honest with them. More important, they will appreciate you for trusting them to be able to cope with your saying "no."

SHIFTING GEARS FROM RESPONSIVE I-MESSAGES TO ACTIVE LISTENING

Not infrequently when you say "no" to others, even in the most effective, sensitive way possible, they are going to have a negative reaction, especially if you've always said "yes" to them before.

Recall that an essential attitude underlying your use of I-Messages is your willingness and ability to shift gears to Active Listening if you see the other person has a problem with what you say. As you learn to send stronger I-Messages, it becomes increasingly essential for you to shift gears and listen, so you can hear resistance, understand it, and show your empathy for needs that the other feels are being threatened.

Notice how gears are shifted in this situation sent in by an E.T.W. participant:

"Pete often needs typing done when his secretary is out of the office. He's been asking me to help him out, and I've always done so. Recently, I decided I didn't want to continue to do this extra work. The conversation went as follows."

Pete: Nancy, would you type this report for me? My secretary is out today.

Nancy: No, Pete. I've decided I don't want to do these typing jobs for you anymore. It's not part of my job.

Pete: What's with you today? You've always done it before.

Nancy: My reaction today really surprises you. (SHIFTING GEARS WITH ACTIVE LISTENING)

Pete: Yeah—I thought we were friends and that you liked helping me out.

Nancy: My saying "no" makes you wonder about our relationship—and whether I've been phony. (ACTIVE LISTENING)

Pete: Yeah.

Nancy: No, Pete, I do like you and do want to continue to be friends. I'd just like to stop doing work I don't get paid for.

USING RESPONSIVE I-MESSAGES TO SAY "YES"

You can also use the Responsive I-Message when you want to say "yes" to an acceptable request from another person. Becoming aware of (and giving your reasons for) saying "yes" helps you keep in touch with your honest feelings, and tells the other person you're honoring the request because you really want to; it lets her or him know that you aren't reluctantly giving in. This kind of positive self-disclosure promotes openness and positive feelings between people, as in these examples:

"Yes, I'd like to hand out campaign posters for Lorraine Nelson. I believe strongly in what she stands for, and I'd like to help her."

"Yes, I'd really like to come for lunch tomorrow. I've really missed talking to you lately."

"Yes, I'd enjoy helping you make dinner. I love you and I like doing nice things for you."

"Yes, I'd be glad to help you get your work out this week. That'll give me a chance to repay you for things you've done for me."

"Yes, I'd like to go to your meeting tomorrow night. It'll give me a chance to understand more about what you're involved in."

When you learn to send Responsive I-Messages (either "yes" or "no") to requests from others, remember that the most important consideration is that you are sure you're keeping in balance your concern for yourself and your concern for others.

V. HOW TO PREVENT SOME CONFLICTS

One's self grows from the consequence of being.

SIDNEY JOURARD

THOUGH they feel a sense of frustration, a lack of fulfillment in their lives, many people never really come to grips with the reasons for their negative feelings. They envy others who seem to be leading productive lives, but they rationalize (a favorite excuse is "bad luck" or "that's the way things go for me") to account for their own lack of achievement and satisfaction.

Often, this lack of satisfaction can be traced directly to a person's inability to communicate wants and needs clearly and congruently. Learning to use Responsive I-Messages helps to deal honestly with requests that you really want to turn down, and puts you more in control of how you spend your time and energy. Obviously, getting free of unacceptable tasks, burdens, and obligations is a major milestone toward personal freedom.

But freedom *from*—from spending your time in dissatisfying and unfulfilling ways—is only half the answer. The other half is freedom *to*—to apply your time, energy, and talents in ways that are meaningful to you and will lead toward the achievement of your goals. Your pursuit of this positive form of freedom will necessarily place you in situations in which you need understanding, support, cooperation, or participation from other people. If you want others' cooperation when you need it, the relationship must feel reciprocal to them—they must feel you are willing to help them meet their needs. Your relationships with others will always go through many changes and reversals; you'll be able to give help on one occasion, another time you'll seek it. In all such life changes your most reliable guide is your ability to stay in touch with your needs and values, always remembering to remain sensitive to those of others.

PREVENTIVE I-MESSAGES

When you have a need that requires some form of cooperation or support of another person, your full disclosure of that need is what we call the Preventive I-Message. It is a self-disclosure that involves you in a shared experience with people with whom you have relationships, and who can help you get your needs met. Like all I-Messages, it is an assertive expression, clear and direct, avoiding both nonassertive and aggressive overtones. Remember that other people are better able and willing to help you meet your needs if they have a clear picture of what you want.

The Preventive I-Message is so named because it can *prevent* many conflicts and misunderstandings—your message lets others know ahead of time what you will need and want. Informing others of your needs helps them stay closely involved with you, keeps them from being surprised later on, and prepares them for possible changes you might want to make that might affect them.

An E.T.W. participant describes her effective use of Preventive I-Messages with mothers in her group:

"I give lots of time to various groups such as Brownies, PTA, etc. I have a younger child, and I was spending a lot of money for baby-sitting and fretting over the expense. I was becoming resentful that I was always the one who says 'yes,' while the other mothers stayed home. My main resentment was the amount of money I was spending. I sent a self-disclosure [PRE-VENTIVE I-MESSAGE] to some other parents about the extra expense, and a request that they watch my younger son while I was busy helping their children. The outcome was that I could still volunteer my time and enjoy helping, without the worry about baby-sitting expenses, because the other mothers were very willing to watch my son."

Another E.T.W. participant describes a conversation she had with her parents:

"Lately I've felt obligated to go to my hometown for Christmas and visit my parents—and this year decided to stay at home. I expressed my feelings to them (guilt), and my need to stay put and visit them other times during the year. I learned that all this time they had insisted I spend Christmas with them because they were afraid I'd feel lonely! They appeared relieved at not having to 'entertain,' and plan to take a little trip instead."

Another tells of her experience with her family:

"I get home after work tired, and not feeling up to preparing supper right away. Everybody's hungry! I talked to all three in my family and told them that, just as they get tired at work or at school, I feel the same way; that, with cooperation, after a short rest we could all help prepare supper, or maybe they could start something if they were not too tired themselves. Now when I get home supper is started sometimes, the house is tidied up (good feeling!), and sometimes either my husband or my oldest son takes us out to dinner."

We find again and again that as women learn to use skills of effective self-disclosure, they are astonished and delighted at the newfound cooperativeness of other people. They grow to realize that potential acceptance, support, or helpfulness has been available all along, in others as well as in themselves. They just remained dormant. A bit of dialogue that strikes a familiar chord with many people is:

"But I didn't know you felt that way! Why didn't you tell me?"

"You never asked."

How many unmet needs, unfulfilled relationships, and unrealized goals can be traced to the fact that "you never asked," or asked too late, or asked in a way that turned people off instead of giving them a chance to act out their friendship by being cooperative?

An effective Preventive I-Message generally consists of two parts:

1. Your self-disclosure (assertion) of your need

"I want to go back to school."

"I need some rest."

"I'd like to have some fun."

"I would appreciate it if we could stay home this weekend."

"I've decided I'd like to get a better job."

2. The reasons for the need (desired consequence)

"I want . . . because . . ."

It's important to state the reasons for your need so your message won't sound authoritarian or aggressive. It's not hard to guess how your spouse will react if you tell him:

"I've decided to go back to work, so I want your help with the household chores!"

Using the Preventive I-Message, you might say instead:

"I've decided to go back to work because I'd like to help with the increasing expenses we have. Also, I need productive work to do that gives me a chance to use my college training. And I'm going to need help with the household chores."

The first message comes across as too aggressive and demanding; the second as a carefully thought out self-disclosure.

You'll find it won't be easy to send Preventive I-Messages successfully unless:

You know what you want or need, and why.

You decide to take personal responsibility for meeting your need.

You can express your need in an assertive way to the person whose cooperation you need.

You're willing to shift gears to listening if the other person becomes defensive.

Preventive I-Messages are particularly useful when someone has previously blocked you in meeting your needs and you want to try again with a clearer message; and with someone with whom you have no previous experience (you'll want to make certain you don't come across as aggressive or demanding).

Our experience has proven that the Preventive I-Message has many advantages, not only for you but for those with whom you are involved. Among them are:

You maintain awareness, responsibility, and control of your needs and feelings.

Others learn what your needs are, and the strength of your feelings about them.

You are an example of openness, directness, congruence, thereby encouraging reciprocal behavior by others.

You reduce the chances of future conflicts and tensions from unknown or uncommunicated needs, thus decreasing the element of surprise that often jolts even the closest relationships.

You take full responsibility for the plans you've made, and you prepare for future needs.

Your relationships stay healthy, because they're based on openness and honesty.

Here are some examples of good Preventive I-Messages:

"I'd like to set up a time to meet with you to plan what we're going to do at the conference, so I'll feel prepared and less anxious when we get there."

"I'd like you to tell me when you don't plan to come home after school, so I don't get worried about you."

"I'd like us to figure out what needs to be done before we leave for the weekend, so we make sure we have time to get it all done."

"I'd like to know when you'll bring the kids back, because I've made plans for the day."

"I'd like to know what we're going to discuss in our meeting tomorrow, so I can bring the necessary information with me."

"I'd like to know when we're having dinner, because there's a long phone call I want to make."

AVOIDING YOU-MESSAGES

Declarative, Responsive, and Preventive I-Messages are all expressions of who you are and what you think, feel, value, or need. They tell others what's going on inside you and help to create a climate of cooperation rather than resistance. They reflect your awareness of yourself and your desire to translate this awareness into action. Since they express *your* internal experience, they do not offer judgments or interpretations of the *other's* feelings or behavior.

Too often when we want to communicate our feelings and needs, our messages put down or blame the other person. We call these "You-Messages"; they're negative judgments or evaluations aimed at the other person. While they are most often used to express anger, embarrassment, fear, or hurt, they are definitely not self-disclosing messages, because they do not express your own feelings, needs, or interests. Regardless of how they're intended, You-Messages also come through as aggressive and accusatory, because they say, in effect: "It's your fault!" or "You're to blame!" They risk damaging a relationship by diminishing the other's self-esteem and producing feelings of guilt.

What are *your* reactions when people send You-Messages such as these?

"You're late."

"You're *so* lazy!"

"Why are you so mean?"

"You're inconsiderate."

"You're so bossy."

"You're messy."

"You're crazy."

"I can't believe how irresponsible you are!"

"You should pull your weight more around the house."

"You should check with me before making decisions."

For many people, it comes as a shock when they discover for the first time how much of their normal conversation is filled with You-Messages. They have always been under the impression that they were honestly saying what was on their minds! "The last thing I would ever want to do," they insist, "is make anyone feel guilty. I've had enough of that done to me!" Then why are You-Messages so common?

As in saying "yes" when we mean "no," it seems easier to express ourselves in You-Messages. They roll more readily off the tongue, because they require no self-awareness and shift responsibility from ourselves to others. They are also an easy, impulsive way to get back at people when they hurt us. Some additional problems of You-Messages:

You don't take responsibility for your own feelings.

You usually don't accomplish your purpose; in fact, You-Messages cause resistance and defensiveness in others.

They can start destructive arguments or name-calling.

They cause the other person to feel bad, put down, criticized, hurt.

The other person often feels like getting back at you, retaliating.

They communicate a lack of respect for the feelings of the other person.

Because it is so important to avoid You-Messages in relationships, let's identify some typical You-Messages and contrast them with I-Messages in the same situations:

Situation	You-Message	I-Message
You would like to celebrate your anniversary this year.	"You *never* take me to dinner on our anniversary."	"I'd really enjoy celebrating our anniversary at a restaurant this year instead of having dinner at home."
Your spouse suggests converting extra basement space into a game room.	"How thoughtless can you get! You know I've been planning to use the space for my darkroom."	"I've really been counting on that space for my darkroom."
A coworker frequently uses the company's only conference room.	"You have no right to monopolize the conference room."	"I have some important meetings coming up for which I'll need the conference room. Let's get together and work out a schedule."

Here are additional important points to remember about You-Messages. A You-Message does not automatically turn into an I-Message when it's preceded by "I feel" or "I think." Suppose you say to your coworker:

"I feel you're inconsiderate when you monopolize the only conference room in the building. I think you should realize there are others working here who also need a place for meetings."

Even though you started the message with "I," you're actually saying: "You're inconsiderate and thoughtless; you have little concern for others." Your coworker will understandably feel resentful and will be in no mood to offer you cooperation.

You-Messages also may conceal some emotions that you may need to face up to honestly. In the incident with your coworker, you may feel that she receives more privileges than you do. Underneath that, you may feel unappreciated and undervalued; at a level still further down, you may feel personally inadequate, or dissatisfied with the job itself. When you point a finger at others (rather than search for your own real feelings), you sometimes miss the chance of exploring and gaining deeper understanding of yourself.

SHIFTING GEARS FROM PREVENTIVE I-MESSAGES TO ACTIVE LISTENING

As in all types of self-disclosure, Preventive I-Messages also entail some real risks. You may bring up a subject for which the other person is unprepared, and provoke a defensive reaction. Or you may run into a conflict so profound and potent that it must then be dealt with through more complex and time-consuming problem-solving methods. (The six-step problem-solving method will be discussed in Chapter X.)

When others feel they may have to change or adapt their behavior to you and your needs, it's natural that they may turn resistant. When you do meet with such a reaction, remember how crucial it is to shift immediately from self-disclosure to Active Listening.

An E.T.W. participant wrote out this dialogue of a situation that provoked resistance—and how she handled it:

"I had just started a new job, and was unsure of my responsibilities, so I decided to go to my boss to get some clarification."

Kathleen: I'd like to set up a time for us to meet. I have some things I'd like to discuss with you. (PREVENTIVE I-MESSAGE)

Boss: (Sigh) Oh, really? Can it wait? Is it terribly important?

Kathleen: You sound really hassled. (ACTIVE LISTENING)

Boss: I really am—I have those articles to write, and I'm leaving for the convention next week.

Kathleen: You seem worried and anxious about getting everything done. (ACTIVE LISTENING)

Boss: Yes, that's right.

Kathleen: I hear you, and I really do need to discuss some important issues with you. I'd like us to make an appointment for after you get back, OK? (RE-ASSERTION OF PREVENTIVE I-MESSAGE)

Boss: OK—that would be great. How about early Monday of the week I return?

Joanne, another E.T.W. participant, sent us this report of what happened when she used a Preventive I-Message in her family:

"I was interested in joining a new women's organization that was being formed. This would be something I would have to spend a good deal of time working in. My husband's reaction was immediate concern that I wouldn't have time for the kids, the house would be neglected, would I have time for the things I was already involved in?!!! I used some Active Listening to get further into his real feelings and emotions and cool him off a little."

Joanne: You sound like you're worried that I won't have time for my usual duties.

Husband: Yeah, I am. How are you gonna take care of the kids?

Joanne: You're really concerned about that, aren't you?

Husband: Yes, and how about me? When will *we* ever have time together?

Joanne: I can see you feel kinda threatened by this deal.

Husband: Yes, I do. . . .

"I then reassured him that my husband and my family were my primary concern, and they'd get plenty of care and attention. Then I restated my need to be a part of this new organization. Then he said: 'What did you say this thing was all about?' I explained it, and he said: 'Well, it does sound exciting and like something you'd really enjoy and could contribute to.' So we then looked at the calendar and the actual amount of time I'd be spending, what I'd worked out for the kids, and other planning ahead I'd done. It really works!!'"

Obviously, timing is very important in minimizing the risks and maximizing the effectiveness of Preventive I-Messages. The longer you avoid letting others know about your important needs, the more difficult it will be to accomplish your purpose. That's why we stress the importance of always exploring your needs and values, then translating them into action without unnecessary delays or postponements. Misunderstandings and tensions between people have a way of building up and getting worse over time; then it becomes more complicated to clear them up.

VI. WHO OWNS THE PROBLEM?

Don't give your advice before you are called upon.

ERASMUS

WHILE Preventive I-Messages can deal with conflicts *before* they occur, we all know that many problems in relationships come up suddenly and unexpectedly and cannot be prevented. Also, even the clearest Preventive I-Messages may fail to get the cooperation and support you need. Then your needs aren't met and you have a problem.

Consider, too, what happens when a child, husband, coworker, or friend tells you she or he is having a problem —an unmet need, a hurt, a frustration, a dilemma, a loss. This is a different problem in your relationships—one being experienced by the other person.

Because such problems are so common in *all* relationships—actually, they're inevitable—people who want to maintain rewarding and satisfying relationships in their lives need special skills to recognize when they emerge; define them accurately; and find solutions.

A wide variety of skills is needed. Some work only with one type of problem and not with the others. You'll want to choose the best skill for each kind.

In the E.T.W. course (as in all Effectiveness Training courses), we use a graphic model to help determine which particular skill or set of skills will be most appropriate. We call this model the Behavior Rectangle. Understanding this rectangle will help you organize your thinking about relationship problems—who "owns" the problem (you, the other, or both) and what skills are needed to get the problem resolved.

THE BEHAVIOR RECTANGLE

Start out by thinking of the area within the rectangle below as containing all the behaviors of one person with whom you have a relationship—everything that person says or does. Of course, there will be hundreds of such behaviors, each represented by the letter "B."

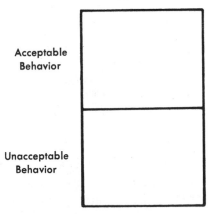

Now let's divide the rectangle into two sections, labeling the top section the Area of Acceptable Behavior and the bottom the Area of Unacceptable Behavior.

Acceptable
Behavior

Unacceptable
Behavior

The top section represents behavior of the other person that you find *acceptable* to you. Acceptable behavior is behavior that does not cause a problem for you. You accept another person's behavior if it does not interfere with your life or with your meeting your needs. At these times you feel good (or neutral) about the other's behavior.

The bottom section represents behavior *not acceptable* to you. Unacceptable behavior is behavior that causes you a problem—it interferes with your life or your efforts to meet your needs and gives you feelings of irritation, fear, discomfort, anger, worry.

Factors That Influence Your Feelings About Another's Behavior

Some people are generally more accepting than others. People who are getting a lot of their personal needs met (and who like themselves) are usually more tolerant of others than people who are unhappy or dissatisfied with their own lives. Regardless of our general level of acceptance, our day-to-day acceptance of others' behavior is influenced by three factors:

The Self

The Environment

The Other Person

Let's discuss each in more detail.

THE SELF

Your mood—your mental and physical state when the behavior takes place—can significantly influence your attitude toward that behavior. Suppose you had a wonderful morning—you feel really happy—so when your boss hands you some rush work, you feel fine about doing it. If you got up with a persistent headache, you'd probably find the rush job really unacceptable. If you feel great, the boss's behavior is above your acceptance line. If you feel bad, the same behavior falls below your line, as illustrated here:

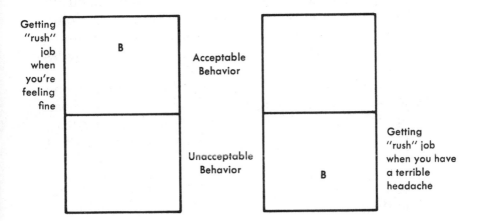

THE ENVIRONMENT

The time and place of a behavior is also crucial. It may be fine with you for your child to ride her bike on the quiet streets of your neighborhood but unacceptable for

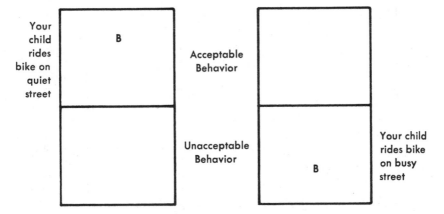

her to ride on streets with heavy traffic. In a work situation, you may be entirely accepting of a coworker's telling you about her separation during your lunch hour, but highly unaccepting during working hours.

THE OTHER PERSON

How you feel about a behavior is inevitably influenced by who the person is and how you feel about her or him. Your reaction to each person is a complex amalgam of impressions, sensations, prior experiences, snap judgments, deep-seated values, thoughtful appraisal, biases, prejudices, stereotypes, preferences. If you label someone by a category (fat, egghead, extrovert, male chauvinist, loner, swinger, freeloader), that can touch off negative vibrations in you—or readily win your approval. All of which means you like some people better than others. Obviously, you can feel accepting of a behavior in one person and unaccepting if someone else does exactly the same thing.

If a close friend phones you at an inconvenient time, you'll probably find this acceptable and might put aside whatever you're doing to talk to your friend. If someone you dislike calls when you're busy, you'll be far less accepting—very likely you'll cut the conversation short.

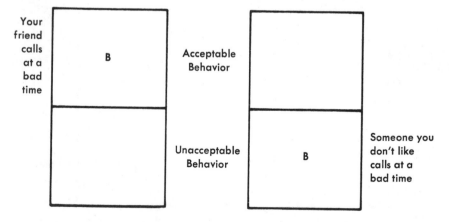

These three influencers—self, environment, and the other person—shift and interact in an infinite number of ways to determine what *is* acceptable and what is *not* acceptable to you. So the line dividing the two areas is continually moving up and down.

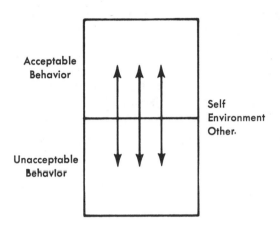

PROBLEM OWNERSHIP

The Behavior Rectangle is a vehicle for explaining another important concept—problem ownership.

It's an idea that may seem strange at first. People think of problems as existing outside of themselves—in other people, in the environment, in the circumstances, in the system. Or we think of ownership of tangible things: we own a house, a car, a television set. How can we own something as intangible as a human problem, and why is it important to think about problems in those terms?

Problem ownership is an especially important idea for women, who so often have been in the position of trying to solve everyone's problems—their husbands', parents', bosses', and particularly children's—to the point that they often take on others' problems as though the problems were their own. We tend to lose sight of the fact that each of us has needs and goals unique and separate from those of others. Let's take a more detailed look at problem ownership and how it functions in relationships.

When There Is No Problem in the Relationship

We have been dealing only with behavior of others that is generally acceptable to you—situations in which the other person's behavior is in the upper part of the Behavior Rectangle, the Area of Acceptable Behavior. You feel accepting toward the other person's behavior because it's not interfering with your life—it doesn't cause you a problem. You can function effectively in ways that meet your needs. In the rectangle, let's label the top section the No-Problem Area.

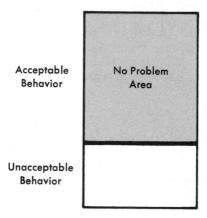

Acceptable
Behavior

No Problem
Area

Unacceptable
Behavior

Some examples of situations in the No-Problem Area might be:

Your husband and you are having an exciting, stimulating discussion.

Your children are playing quietly; you're reading a book.

Your coworker and you are working together in a productive, satisfying way.

Whenever the other person's behavior falls into the No-Problem Area of your rectangle, you're free to pursue your own goals or, in a conversation, express your ideas, opinions, wants, needs. Because you feel accepting of the other, you'll probably be in the mood to listen and to understand. You'll be using all the skills discussed in the previous chapters: Declarative I-Messages, Responsive I-Messages, Preventive I-Messages, Shifting Gears to Active Listening.

When You Own the Problem

Obviously, whenever the other person's behavior is interfering (or has *already* interfered) with your meeting your needs and you start feeling troubled, upset, worried, or angry, you don't feel accepting of the other's behavior, so you own the problem. On the Behavior Rectangle the "You Own the Problem" area is below your acceptance line.

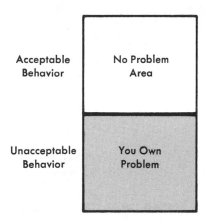

Acceptable Behavior — No Problem Area

Unacceptable Behavior — You Own Problem

Here are some situations in which you own the problem:

The person who shares your office is a heavy smoker, and the smoke makes you cough and sneeze.

You're being detained by your supervisor and miss a dental appointment, which you must pay for anyway.

Your daughter plays her stereo at a very high volume, making it difficult for you to concentrate.

You're being prevented from meeting your needs, so you'd like the other person to change her or his unacceptable behavior. To solve this problem you need to take the initiative.

An effective way of increasing the chances she or he will change is through confrontation: strong, forceful self-disclosure. Deciding to confront others when they interfere with your meeting your needs is an effective way of assuming responsibility for getting some of your problems solved.

When Both Own the Problem

Sometimes it becomes apparent that you and the other person have a joint problem or a conflict (the relationship owns a problem). Both of you are experiencing feelings of unacceptance and dissatisfaction in your relationship. The existence of a conflict usually becomes evident when one of you expresses your unmet needs, or confronts the other person. We show such conflicts in the bottom part of the rectangle:

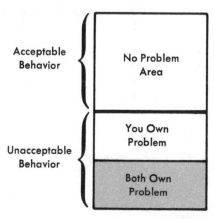

Acceptable Behavior { No Problem Area

Unacceptable Behavior { You Own Problem

Both Own Problem

Some examples are:

Your husband wants to have a baby and you don't.

You feel you deserve a raise; your boss disagrees.

Your child wants to have a pet very badly and you don't.

Situations such as these require skills of conflict resolution, which will be dealt with in Chapters X and XI.

When the Other Person Owns the Problem

The other person owns the problem when she or he is experiencing unhappiness or dissatisfaction in her or his own life, quite independently of you. Because it has no real or tangible effect on you, you can accept the behavior. You may want to help the other person or you may not. Still, you do not own the problem, so you can remain separate from it.

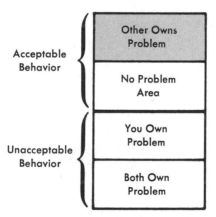

Here are some problems owned by the other person:

Your daughter is having problems with her schoolwork.

Your husband is about to retire and is anxious about ways to use his
    time.

Your friend is unhappy with her job.

It can be a relieving, freeing experience to leave owner-ship with another person. It means you need no longer assume responsibility for solving problems for her or him. Other advantages are:

You are relieved of the pressure of feeling you need to have all the answers.

You allow others to solve their own problems, which helps them gain independence, responsibility, and confidence in their own percep-tions and judgments.

The other side of the coin of assuming responsibility for your own life, needs, problems is allowing others the freedom to do the same.

Your solutions are often not what's best for another person.

Giving people solutions to their problems carries the risk that they will blame you if your solutions don't work.

It's difficult to know what lies beneath a problem presented by another person. If you jump in right away with your solutions you may prevent the person from getting in touch with a deeper feeling or problem.

Taking over another's problems and offering solutions can make her or him increasingly dependent on you.

An E.T.W. participant recognized her own tendencies to solve her children's problems:

"I've always felt that parents should have answers for their children to help them solve their problems, but realize that it's a mistake to not let them solve their own; give them freedom to express themselves, but also lend them support."

In Chapter XIII we will show you how you can play an active role in helping another person solve her or his own problem without offering solutions, giving advice, or taking responsibility away from the person.

DIFFERENT SKILLS FOR DIFFERENT PROBLEMS

The Behavior Rectangle is a visual picture of your relationship with a particular person; the problems that can occur; and a reminder that ownership of problems can rest with you, with the other person, or with both of you. This concept of ownership is of critical importance, because certain skills are called for when you own the problem; others when the other person owns the problem; and still others when both share the problem. The following chart contrasts the three postures for the three different kinds of problems.

When You Own the Problem	When the Other Owns the Problem
You use the confrontation skills	You use the helping skills
You take responsibility for getting your needs met	You leave responsibility with the other for meeting her/his needs
You initiate communication	The other initiates communication
You are an influencer	You are a counselor
You want to help yourself	You want to help the other person
You want to "sound off"	You are a "sounding board"

When Both Own the Problem
Both are self-disclosing and confrontive
Both need to listen accurately to the other's feelings
Both want to be sensitive to the needs of the other
Both get involved in the problem-solving process
Both take responsibility for offering solutions
Both must find the final solution acceptable

VII. WHEN YOU OWN THE PROBLEM

Anger repressed can poison a relationship as surely as the cruelest words.

JOYCE BROTHERS

. . . Perhaps we have not fully understood that anger is a secondary emotional cover for hurt. (Righteous indignation feels good . . . hurts do not.)

CHARLOTTE PAINTER

YOUR husband continually interrupts you in public.

Your coworker sometimes makes unilateral decisions about issues that affect you.

Your friend has borrowed money and agreed to repay it, but has not.

Your subordinate often comes to work late.

Your boss often doesn't inform you when he will be out of town.

Your child doesn't come home from school on time.

In all these situations, the other person has already behaved in a way that interferes with your needs or rights, so her or his behavior is unacceptable to you.

Preventive I-Messages obviously are inappropriate when the other person has *already* caused you a problem. Now the Confrontive I-Message becomes the self-disclosure skill to use.

The Confrontive I-Message is a constructive way to express negative feelings. Though similar to the other kinds of self-disclosure (it's authentic, congruent, and direct), it is somewhat different and more complex, because you confront the other person with your negative feelings about how her or his behavior affects you.

CONFRONTIVE I-MESSAGES

When another person's behavior is interfering (or has already interfered) with your meeting your needs, *you* own the problem. Now you need to send an I-Message stronger than the ones we discussed earlier. You want to focus on your negative feelings and your unmet needs. And your ultimate purpose is to change the situation so your needs will be met.

Effective confrontation recognizes the other's rights and needs as well as your own, so ideally you want to communicate:

That you'd like to get your needs met, hopefully through a change in the other's behavior

That you want to preserve the other's self-esteem

That you want to maintain the relationship

The chances that the other person will be willing to modify her or his behavior will be greatly increased if your confrontive message contains these elements:

Your feelings

What behavior of hers or his is causing you a problem

How that behavior is affecting you

A message encapsuling these three elements is what we call a Confrontive I-Message. We'll need to go into each in more detail.

Expressing Your Feelings

To increase the chances that the other person will change unacceptable behavior, she or he needs to know how you feel about it. It's not easy to disclose your feelings in Confrontive I-Messages, because negative feelings are tapped, and most of us have been taught to keep them to ourselves. But if you try to keep your feelings in check, you'll only send mixed and confusing messages, and elements of unacceptance are likely to show through.

When you express feelings through Confrontive I-Messages, they should, first of all, be specific and descriptive. They should match as closely as possible the intensity of your emotional level. If you're really angry, it's not advisable to hold back and sound as though you're mildly annoyed ("It doesn't matter much" or "I hope it won't cause you any bother, but . . ."). Underplaying your feelings won't give other people the information they need for understanding how their behavior is affecting you. Overplaying your emotions is equally misleading. If you put on a show of anger greater than you feel, just to make your point, your message may come across as an overreaction. The other person, not sure where you really stand, will not be inclined to make changes, and will learn not to trust your authenticity at later times.

It's important to keep a clear emotional focus and be sure the feeling you express is the true one. Because feelings operate on more than one level, it's often difficult to achieve clarity. Anger, probably the most common feeling in confrontation, is often the result of another feeling that reflects a more basic, underlying need.

Anger is often a way of retaliating, a way of getting back

at someone who has hurt us. It is often a secondary feeling, which covers up deeper, more vulnerable feelings such as fear, rejection, hurt, or embarrassment. It is often easier for us to express anger at others than to let them know how vulnerable we are—how afraid or hurt or rejected we feel by what they said or did.

If your spouse is unusually late returning from work, and you've been worrying about a possible car accident, when he finally arrives home after having stopped off for a drink with a colleague, you may explode, "Why didn't you call me? How can you be so inconsiderate? Dinner is ruined!" This message does not express your more basic feeling of fear. A more congruent I-Message would be something like: "I was really worried that something had happened to you—I'm so glad you're home safe!"

Not that anger should never be expressed—in fact, venting angry feelings can often help you get in touch with your deeper feelings. After the anger gets out, it's easier to focus on your hurt or rejection.

Anger is a normal reaction when someone gets prevented from meeting her or his needs. Many women, in particular, have the continuing experience of being blocked in meeting many of their important needs, partly because of cultural stereotypes, restrictions, discrimination, and the like.

We have been taught that anger is bad—we should not feel it; and if we do, certainly we should not express it. Because other people react so negatively to anger and other negative feelings, we try to suppress them. However, since we cannot deny these feelings, we must deal with them somehow. This is why so many women communicate anger indirectly rather than face the consequences of open confrontation.

Some of the indirect ways women have learned for venting anger are:

Getting sick—having headaches, developing asthma

Getting depressed, feeling bored, restless, anxious

Making sarcastic remarks

Withdrawing from relationships

Complaining to a third party

Putting others down, criticizing, ridiculing, blaming

Giving people the "silent treatment"

Sabotaging other people's efforts when they try to get their needs met

We also know that when anger can no longer be contained, people blow up and explode. Since this has often been our only experience with anger, it's no wonder we're so afraid to express it.

All these reactions are self-destructive and ineffective for you individually and for your relationships with others. They don't help you take responsibility for your feelings. Indirect ways of expressing anger take a great deal of physical and mental energy that could better be spent facing anger directly. Also, relationships suffer a lot more in the long run if anger is suppressed or expressed indirectly, rather than openly expressed.

Developing a new way of thinking about (and handling) anger is critical. To start, we need to:

Recognize and accept our anger

Allow ourselves to feel it

Learn to express it in ways that don't damage relationships we value

Try to get more in touch with the underlying feelings anger sometimes represents

You need not be afraid of your anger, and need not think of it as abnormal and unhealthy. You have a right to feel angry when your needs are blocked. Learning to accept anger as a valid emotion or reaction is the first step in coming to terms with it. Only when you treat it that way can you begin to understand it, explore it, grow from it. When you don't express it openly and congruently, it gets mixed up indistinguishably with all negative feelings.

As women gain the courage to express anger in authentic, nonblameful ways, they discover that many other feelings are involved. Anger is only the most obvious, the one closest to the surface. We can never discover, experience, and come to terms with other underlying negative feelings—and many resulting positive feelings—until we have the courage to express our anger.

Granted, expressing anger in relationships is difficult and may not be a pleasant experience for either person, but it's far better than bottling it up—getting sick, having depressions, feeling constantly resentful, and ultimately damaging or destroying relationships instead of talking and negotiating your way to better understanding.

Obviously, not all feelings you get when someone's behavior is causing you a problem are anger. When our needs are frustrated or when there is the threat of not getting our needs met, we may get a wide variety of feelings: fear, sorrow, worry, disappointment, regret, hurt, rejection, embarrassment, jealousy, annoyance, irritation, and many more. The key to clear communication of such feelings is your ability to identify your own feelings and express them as I-Messages:

"I'm really disappointed."

"I'm afraid."

"I'm worried."

"I feel annoyed."

When you can start your confrontation with such I-Messages, you're truly self-disclosing—revealing what is going on inside you instead of blaming the other person for causing you a problem, as these You-Messages do:

"You really disappointed me."

"You made me afraid."

"You worried me."

"You're annoying me."

Let's describe a situation in which you're developing negative feelings because the behavior of another person is interfering with your needs. We'll use it to begin illustrating how to send a good three-part Confrontive I-Message.

Arrangements have been made for you to share an office with a colleague with whom you will be working closely on an important project. You soon become aware that your coworker spends a lot of time on the telephone discussing personal and family business. You realize he's in the middle of difficult family problems. You try to be accepting of this behavior. However, you become increasingly resentful as you find that the telephone conversations interfere with your ability to concentrate, and you're forced to take over many of his tasks because of the time absorbed by his frequent personal conversations.

Your Confrontive I-Message might start out like this:

"I'm worried because . . ."

"I'm feeling really frustrated and annoyed . . ."

"I'm scared that . . ."

"I'm upset . . ."

Describing What Behavior Is Causing You a Problem

This part of the Confrontive I-Message simply describes the other's unacceptable behavior: what she or he is doing that bothers you, _not_ your label or judgment of that behavior. When another person's behavior interferes with your needs, it's really easy and tempting to put down the other person with blaming You-Messages. As we've said, You-Messages make the other person defensive, resentful, and upset; and they have much less chance of influencing the other to change.

Let's contrast some nonblameful descriptions of behavior with You-Messages:

Nonblameful Description of Other's Behavior	_Judgmental You-Messages_
Your husband interrupts you.	"You're inconsiderate."
Your child doesn't come home from school and doesn't call.	"You're irresponsible."
Your coworker doesn't consult you about decisions affecting you.	"You don't care about me or my opinions."

In the case of your coworker who is on the telephone all the time, it probably won't work to say "I'm frustrated and annoyed because you're inconsiderate." Tell him only what he is doing that interferes with you: "I'm frustrated and annoyed _when you spend so much time on the phone._"

Think of it this way: your only purpose is to bring about a change in his behavior, not to punish him or make him feel guilty or embarrassed. What you want is to continue your work and also to maintain your relationship. Describing only his unacceptable behavior has a far better chance to succeed than a message of criticism that might make him defensive or resistant.

Explaining How That Behavior Affects You

The third part of an effective Confrontive I-Message is an honest statement of the consequences of the other's behavior. How does the behavior affect you or interfere with your life?

It might cost you time, energy, or money you would rather spend somewhere else.

It might prevent you from doing something you need or want to do.

It might physically hurt you, make you work harder, make you tired, cause you pain or discomfort.

These are tangible, concrete consequences—effects that others can readily understand. The intangible consequences to you would include such effects as worry, fear, anxiety, embarrassment, disappointment.

The other person is much more likely to change her or his behavior if she or he is told how it affects you, so it's especially important not to leave out the tangible effects. Most people can understand and accept this information. Intangible effects, on the other hand, can sometimes invite such dismissals as:

"You're such a worrywart."

"Stop being afraid."

"I don't see why you need to be disappointed."

"Everything makes you nervous."

When your coworker who phones so much hears from you: "I'm frustrated and annoyed when you spend so much time on the phone *because I can't concentrate and my work isn't getting done,*" it's clear to him how his behavior affects you, and it greatly increases the chances he'll modify his behavior.

Here are some other good examples of effective three-part Confrontive I-Messages:

To Husband: I feel hurt when you interrupt me, because I don't get to finish my point, and it makes me feel you don't care about what I have to say.

To Coworker: I'm really angry that I wasn't consulted about the price increases, because they affect my department and its income.

To Friend: I'm upset because you didn't pay me back like we agreed, because I was counting on having the money for something else.

To Subordinate: I'm really fed up with your coming in late so often. [Because] I don't like paying you for time you don't work.

To Boss: I get annoyed and frustrated when you don't tell me when you'll be gone, because I can't schedule the work I do for other staff members.

To Child: I get really worried when you don't come home from school on time, and then I get distracted from my work.

When a Confrontive I-Message works, it's for three good reasons: the other person has some degree of concern about how her or his behavior affects you; she or he becomes convinced that the behavior has an effect (tangible and/or intangible) on you; the other person's need to continue the behavior is either not very strong or can be met another way. In other words, if the other person cares about you, understands your problem, realizes what your needs are, and has not been put in a defensive position or made to feel manipulated, she or he will probably be motivated to change the behavior to help you out.

This new behavior may be exactly what you had hoped for, or it could take an unexpected form. If you've been counting on an afternoon nap and your children are carrying on a very loud argument, your Confrontive I-Message may cause them to voluntarily give up the argument and play separately—exactly what you'd expected. They may also surprise you with a solution of their own: moving to the garage, where they can continue arguing without disturbing you.

When an unexpected solution meets your needs without bringing on new problems, it should be welcomed, and such behavior encouraged in the future. If it does not meet your needs, you're still free to turn it down, but with an acknowledgment of the other person's initiative and thoughtfulness.

At times confrontation may strain a relationship, particularly when the elements of conflict have been smoldering for some time. But the result will still probably be an improvement. An E.T.W. participant offered this appraisal of her confrontation with her mother-in-law:

"My own self-esteem as a person increased; my hidden anger decreased. The relationship has become estranged, but that's really more positive than the hostility I held inside me all those years."

SHIFTING GEARS DURING CONFRONTATION

Remember about shifting gears when another person responds defensively to your I-Messages? You should be even more prepared to encounter defensiveness and resistance in confrontation situations (even when your I-Messages contain the three essential elements), because nobody likes to hear that her or his behavior is unacceptable and affects another's life negatively.

In the case of your being distracted and upset by your coworker's personal telephone calls, the dialogue might go something like this:

You: I'm finding it really frustrating and difficult to concentrate when you're talking on the telephone, and I'm concerned about finishing this project by the deadline without your help.

Coworker: I'm concerned about the project too, but I'm also concerned about other things. This job isn't my whole life, you know.

You: I guess you're saying there are other problems in your life right now that have higher priority.

Coworker: Right! Sometimes it's difficult to juggle family and work problems.

You: This must be a very trying time for you.

Coworker: It's driving me up a wall! My younger sister is going through a divorce and there are problems with the kids, and—look, I don't want to bore you with my family troubles.

You: It sounds as though your sister is really depending on you.

Coworker: We've always been very close. But after all, it isn't
             your problem . . . and the project is important to
             me. I'm going to tell her to cut down on the calls.
             I can call her from downstairs during my breaks.

In such a situation, you may shift several times from
Confrontive I-Messages to Active Listening, as feelings on
both sides are shared.

Quite frequently, your self-disclosing confrontation and
listening will bring on a conflict or point up the existence
of one that neither of you had realized existed. Then you
need conflict-resolution skills, and we deal with those in
Chapters IX and X.

VIII. DEALING WITH ANXIETY

The positive aspects of selfhood develop as the individual
confronts, moves through and overcomes anxiety-creating
experiences.

ROLLO MAY

In describing the effective person, we have emphasized the importance of self-knowledge and understanding, taking responsibility for your own life, and communicating your needs, wants, and problems in I-Messages that clearly state your position without blaming or accusing others.

At this point it may seem not only possible but easy for you to send the different self-disclosing messages, and to shift gears to listening; you probably know *how* to be self-disclosing. So why is such a seemingly simple process often so difficult to carry out?

The main obstacle to self-disclosure is anxiety: we become so overwhelmed by feelings of anxiety that we're incapacitated, immobilized.

New possibilities always involve some degree of anxiety. The prospect of becoming a more authentic self-disclosing person, taking responsibility for your own life and for relating to others, is anxiety-provoking because *you can't know the outcomes.* Anxiety is so directly related to effectiveness that it's important to understand its role. Then you can control it and take more responsibility for your life.

WHAT IS ANXIETY?

Anxiety is fear, apprehension, distress, discomfort, or uneasiness that comes over us when we perceive some threat to personal security. Feelings of anxiety are a signal: a problem needs to be solved; something is wrong; we need to do something to regain psychological equilibrium.

Since anxiety is such a painful feeling, we have been taught to try to avoid, ignore, escape from, and deny it. All of us have had the experience of trying to handle anxiety in these ways and know they don't work very well. Feelings of anxiety don't go away. In fact, they become worse the longer we fail to face up to them and deal with them effectively.

Think about times when you've come away from an encounter feeling much worse because the courage to act deserted you. How many lost opportunities can you recall, how many chances for friendship or love, for jobs or interesting new experiences, that slipped by because you were unable to say what you were feeling? The words that might have made all the difference remained unspoken, trapped inside you by doubt and confusion. "I panicked" is how you think of it later. The saddest words in the language, as someone said, are "It might have been," and anxiety is often responsible for these missed opportunities.

We all know that feelings of anxiety have physical manifestations as well: sweaty palms, clammy forehead, perspiring underarms; shaky hands or knees; a fluttering in the pit of the stomach; tension in the neck muscles, lips, jaws, or temples; a shaky or breaking voice; rapid heartbeat; dryness in the mouth; fast, shallow breathing; indigestion, migraine headaches, fatigue. In these states, we're really unable to do what we want to do or have satisfying relationships. An E.T.W. participant described her experience with anxiety this way:

"I came from a nondemonstrative family where no one ever directly expressed how they thought or felt. As a child I learned to tell my parents what they wanted to hear. I let them make my decisions, and I fulfilled their expectations of what I should be. I carried this behavior into my marriage, and for seven years I tried to live up to the role of the 'perfect wife.' My husband's job required him to be gone for extended periods, often months at a time. During those times alone I began to realize that 'I' didn't exist, that all my life I'd been an extension or reflection of someone else. I became very confused by the feelings I was having. I tried to suppress them because I felt guilty for having them. Why should I be so angry and resentful when I had everything? I began to have migraine headaches, numbness in my face, hands and feet; I couldn't sleep; I'd hide in the closet so my child wouldn't hear me crying. I began to go from doctor to doctor, convinced that I had a terminal illness like brain tumors or multiple sclerosis. When all tests were negative, I feared that I was mentally ill. Fortunately, I was referred to a therapist who told me I was having 'anxiety attacks.' Since I was unable to verbally express my intense feelings, my body expressed them for me in frightening physical symptoms. As I began to learn to identify my feelings, accept them, and express them appropriately, the physical symptoms disappeared."

Many people minimize the significance of anxiety and its effects on them. They assume that if they continue with their daily routine and don't deal with what is causing the anxiety, the feelings will eventually go away and they can go back to living as though the feelings had not occurred. If this could happen, it would not be *so* essential to deal with anxiety by facing it directly. The fact is that such feelings don't automatically subside. And when we don't solve the problems that set off anxiety, the consequences can be quite serious, as the preceding example demonstrates. If you continually fail to heed the warning signal of anxiety, you're likely to respond more and more often in inauthentic ways—not being yourself. Eventually you could gradually lose touch with yourself and the rest of the world.

LOOKING AT ANXIETY POSITIVELY

Instead of allowing anxiety to incapacitate you, you can turn it into an opportunity for growth. It's even possible to get pleasantly excited when you feel anxious, because it signals a challenge to move onto a new level.

In his book *The Concept of Dread* Kierkegaard states that "anxiety is always to be understood as directed toward freedom." Freedom is the goal of personality development, and Kierkegaard defines freedom as possibility. But whenever you visualize possibility, anxiety is part of the experience. The more possibility, the greater the potential anxiety. Selfhood depends on the capacity to confront anxiety and move through it in an effective way.

To treat the presence of anxiety as an opportunity for positive growth, it helps to focus on anxiety in a different, more effective way. Here are three useful steps:

1. *Recognize and Accept the Anxiety.*
Keep in mind that anxiety signals a possibility for you to grow, to expand—a potential opportunity for you to develop. Become excited and motivated by its existence. It *can* be confronted in a constructive way.

2. *Decide to Act to Solve the Problem That Triggers Anxiety.*
Think of constructive ways the anxiety can be confronted. Decide to take a risk. You stand to gain, because in the long run the risk is often much greater if you fail to act in an effective, responsible way. Even though you risk failure or disapproval from others, the price you pay in self-worth for deciding not to act is much higher.

3. *Act to Solve the Problem.*

It's not enough to think about it, to intellectualize about how good you'd feel if you did something—you must act. Once again, strength and courage come if you act. You'll become motivated to work through other anxiety-creating situations.

For your relationships with others, moving through anxiety-creating situations has another dimension. Many women today are experiencing anxiety because their view of themselves in relation to others is changing; it no longer conforms to what others have come to expect. Much anxiety is brought about by conflict between how we want to behave and how we think others expect us to behave. We feel we will get their approval if we conform to their expectations; that we risk disapproval if we don't. Women tell us:

"I have changed, but other people have known me the way I used to be, so I still feel a need to act the way I used to when they're around."

"I find it much easier to act like I want to with *new* people."

"It's so hard to change—especially when it feels like nobody wants me to—except me."

Many women find that their fears about disapproval from others are often largely unfounded. They discover that many people admire and respect them more, relate more to them, even like them better when they can summon the courage to be self-disclosing and act in their own behalf. Others admire their courage to take risks and move forward, and even start seeing them as a model for their own behavior. Here's an example from an E.T.W. participant who shares what a friend recently wrote to her:

"I just graduated on Friday from college. What a great high! You may not know it, but it was your perseverance and graduation that got me through a lot of rough spots. It seemed to go by so fast and you were out so quickly that I knew I could do it too."

More important, as you summon the courage to move through more and more difficult situations, you will find yourself much less dependent on the approval and judgment of others. You start trusting your own perceptions, judgments, and feelings more as your ability to move through anxiety-producing situations increases.

YOU CAN CHOOSE HOW TO HANDLE ANXIETY

Every time you feel anxious, you make a choice about how to deal with it. Either you deny the existence of anxiety, try to ignore, avoid, escape it, and hope it will go away—or you recognize its existence and move toward solving the problem that creates the anxiety.

Here are some consequences:

When You Don't Act on Anxiety-Producing Situation	*When You Do Act on Anxiety-Producing Situation*
Choosing not to move through anxiety is a way of not taking responsibility to meet your needs.	Moving through anxiety is an assertive, responsible, effective act.
Problem doesn't get solved; you often feel more and deeper anxiety.	You are authentic, anxiety dissipates; inner turmoil disappears; problems get solved.
Your self-esteem decreases; you are disappointed in yourself; you become angry at yourself.	Your self-esteem, self-confidence increase; you feel good about yourself.
The inner conflict continues; one more failure to act is added, reinforcing old patterns.	You feel motivated to handle other and more difficult situations.

You don't enhance your self-awareness.	You become more self-aware.
You don't grow; you constrict your development; you don't allow yourself to experience something new.	You expand yourself, your possibilities, your self-direction.
You lose opportunities for the emergence of yourself.	You feel creative; new facets of self emerge.
You not only don't avoid conflict, but more conflict can be created.	You solve your inner conflicts and are able to move forward.
You become more withdrawn, less communicative over time.	You become less withdrawn, more communicative over time.

YOUR ANXIETY HIERARCHY

The first step in confronting your anxiety is to create a hierarchy—a priority list—of the anxiety-creating situations in your own life. Make a list of the ten situations in your life that you don't act on because of the anxiety they cause you. First, simply jot down the situations. Then, rank them so that number 1 is the situation causing you the least anxiety (one that you feel relatively sure you can handle now), 2 a situation causing the next least anxiety, and so on; 10 is the situation causing you the most anxiety. These can be all kinds of situations—personal, professional, social, etc.

Here's what an anxiety hierarchy might look like:

1. Telling my friend that I appreciate her

2. Confronting my family about sharing the housework

3. Inviting someone I'd like to get to know to dinner

4. Telling neighbors I don't want to accept their party invitation

5. Starting to air a conflict with my spouse

6. Starting a conversation with a person I don't know

7. Talking to my parents about our relationship

8. Telling someone I feel hurt by what she said

9. Speaking up in an important meeting when I think my view is unpopular

10. Making a speech to a large group

Your own hierarchy will enable you to start on a situation that represents a low level of risk for you. After you've successfully handled the first situation, you can progress to higher levels of risk. These situations on your list will offer many opportunities for you to be self-disclosing. Keep in mind the importance of sending clear, honest, nonblameful I-Messages, and shifting gears to Active Listening when that's called for.

REDUCING ANXIETY

Sometimes you'll find that your level of anxiety is so high that it's impossible for you to act. Nevertheless, it's a fact that anxiety can be reduced to a level that allows us to be self-disclosing and to get our important needs met. Your goal is not to try to eliminate anxiety altogether. That's impossible. It's even undesirable. A certain amount of anxiety is what keeps us motivated to learn, plan, achieve.

It's the counterproductive anxiety we want to bring under control, so we can handle our inner conflicts and plan for personal effectiveness without being restricted by unnecessary worry and tension. And effective reduction of anxiety requires three basic steps: readiness, rehearsal, and relaxation.

Readiness

When you developed your own hierarchy, you probably found that several of the anxiety-producing situations on your list were aggravated by lack of preparation. Most of us can identify with the feeling of panic that comes when we find ourselves in new circumstances or with people we're meeting for the first time. For many people, "having to make a speech" or "being with people who are older and more experienced than I am" is a leading anxiety producer.

Much of the anxiety can be taken out of situations like these by preparing yourself for what lies ahead. Decide what you plan to say or do, when and where you're going to act. Take some time to anticipate the responses of the other person.

Let's say you have decided you're going to ask your employer for a raise. At the thought of it your stomach muscles begin to tighten. Your palms become sweaty. It's a good idea to have a dialogue with yourself:

"What's the worst thing that could happen? Why does this make me so nervous? Is it because I'm not really sure I deserve a raise? Yes, that's probably it. But why do I feel that way? Maybe it's because I don't have a college degree like the others. But a college degree isn't required for this job. And after all, I've just brought in two big contracts . . . and I've been told several times my work is more than satisfactory. I do think I deserve it, and it's long overdue."

Your next step might be to pick the best time and place. You know that if you choose the office during regular working hours, there are likely to be frequent telephone interruptions. So you suggest meeting at breakfast or lunch. You make a rough outline of the points you're planning to present in favor of your request. You collect backup information to support your position. You formulate I-Messages. A confident message like "I feel good about the quality of my work and I'd like to have a raise" is a lot more effective than a defensive "You promised me a raise after six months if my work justified it, and here it's almost a year and . . ."

Give some thought to the possible consequences of your action. Anticipate your boss's possible responses. How will you respond to each one? Be willing to Active Listen when appropriate, to give additional information, to answer questions. Mentally replay the situation until you begin to feel comfortable with it.

Here is an account from a woman in an E.T.W. class that shows the importance of getting ready by thinking ahead:

"My communication with my father had developed a pattern. Whenever I confronted him, I would say something sarcastic, something to hurt him. When he would say something critical —comment on my children's behavior or the 'foolish way' Bob and I spend our money, or the kind of books I read—I would flare up and lash out at him without thinking of what I was saying or why I was saying it. The result was always the same: we'd have a big fight, he'd stalk out, and I'd be left feeling guilty and miserable. Now I stop and think—though it isn't easy—and try to sort out what I'm really feeling and why I'm feeling that way. It's helped me uncover some of the reasons why my father and I have always related the way we have. I'm actively listening to him now and sending congruent messages; I think we're reaching the point where we can work out the conflict and put the relationship on a new basis."

Readiness also requires good personal-time management. If you take on a task or project, schedule your activities realistically. If you're giving a large dinner party in a month, you may want to plan backward from the date; develop a simple flow chart of priorities so you can get ready in easy steps, making sure that the planning and preparation for the party will fit comfortably into your regular schedule.

When you're faced with a large, complex problem, it's a good idea to reduce it to small, manageable components. That way you won't become overwhelmed before you start. An E.T.W. class member told us:

"I've been helped in a real concrete way to overcome the obstacles in front of me by breaking them down into smaller pieces and looking at each calmly and confidently."

Of course, it's not always possible to plan ahead. Many of our most valuable experiences and interactions with others are unplanned and spontaneous. But even when preplanning would be neither possible nor desirable, you can decrease anxiety by taking a few moments to ready yourself so that what you say will be based on what you need. Preparing yourself for what lies ahead allows you to exercise control over what's important to you, rather than letting your life be controlled by others.

Rehearsal

Throughout our lives, we constantly acquire new skills —driving a car, playing tennis, learning a new language —and we accept the fact that mastering these skills will take a certain amount of practice. We can apply this same principle to the learning of interpersonal skills. There is a fairly widespread assumption that interpersonal skills come naturally; that if we fail with people, something must be wrong with us. That's not the case. Communication is complex. It requires dexterity and coordination, and that takes practice.

Rehearsal is following up the readiness step through practice. It's an opportunity to check out a planned approach beforehand rather than afterward (when undesirable results may already have taken place).

Rehearsing your communication may amount to anything from a tryout in front of the mirror for a few moments to a role-playing exercise with one or more people.

A situation such as a job interview or asking for a raise would call for considerable rehearsal. You might ask a friend to role-play the interviewer or boss. Another friend might act as an evaluator. Trying out your planned communication with others gives you the opportunity to receive feedback about the feelings and reactions of the other role-player. You can then adjust your plan. Some people tape-record their planned messages and study them in playback. Whichever technique you use, the combination of practice and evaluation can significantly reduce anxiety by giving you:

An opportunity to release stored-up tension before the actual communication

An improved plan of action as a result of outside feedback

A successful experience that can ease your mind and build up your confidence

Role-play rehearsals can be helpful in many types of situations that are anxiety-producing for you, such as:

Asking a relative for a loan

Complaining in person to a department store about a defective item

Being interviewed for a job

Saying "no" to a friend's unacceptable request

Stating strong views to your male coworkers

Soliciting funds for a charitable organization

Giving a report to your boss

Confronting your spouse, whose behavior has affected you negatively

Making an important speech

Look over your own anxiety hierarchy and decide which situations you might want to rehearse ahead of time.

Relaxation

Since anxiety is a physiological condition, not just a state of mind, it can also be approached directly, by focusing on the physical symptoms that usually accompany worry and tension. The physical manifestations of anxiety can be greatly relieved through muscle relaxation.

Understanding the physical basis of anxiety is helpful in controlling it. It is reassuring to find that you have more control over your body than you may have thought; that just as your body has controlled you by becoming tense, you can control your body by learning how to make it relax. When you have learned to induce deep relaxation, you'll have eliminated the physical sensation of anxiety. Though you may still have some uneasiness about what's ahead of you, the shaky hands, fluttery stomach, and trembly voice will be sufficiently under control so you can proceed with some confidence to act on your plans.

Muscle relaxation consists of alternately tensing and relaxing your muscles. Learning to breathe deeply is another helpful method. You have probably noticed how, when you're nervous, your breathing becomes quick and shallow; soon you're panting, a condition brought on by muscle tension. Since shallow breathing keeps your muscles taut, practicing to breathe deeply is necessary to reduce your anxiety. (For a complete relaxation exercise, refer to the Appendix, page 207.)

In our efforts to overcome anxiety, we should never lose sight of the fact that this condition is usually brought on by internal conflict; that by identifying the conflict, recognizing the anxiety, and deciding to confront it openly, we can move toward a solution.

IX. CONFLICTS: WHO WINS? WHO LOSES?

Conflict is made to look as if it always appears in the image of extremity, whereas, in fact, it is actually the lack of recognition of the need for conflict and provision of appropriate forms for it that lead to danger. This ultimate destructive form is frightening, but it is also not conflict. It is almost the reverse; it is the end result of the attempt to avoid and suppress conflict.

JEAN BAKER MILLER

Wᴇ have dealt with the attitudes and skills of personal self-disclosure and effectiveness, focusing on individual needs—skills to help you build self-confidence, gain self-esteem, and assume personal responsibility. Principally, these skills help you meet *personal* needs, sometimes on your own and sometimes in cooperation with others.

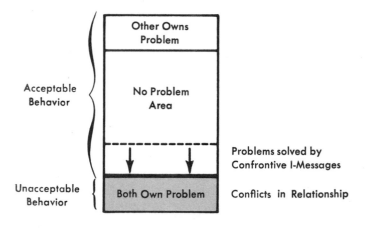

Sometimes you'll find through self-disclosure that another person's needs conflict with yours. Confrontive I-Messages, particularly, can point up such a conflict. It would appear on the Behavior Rectangle as "We Own the Problem" or "The Relationship Owns the Problem."

CONFLICT

What exactly do we mean by "conflict"? The thesaurus provides such synonyms as: "opposition," "flying in the face of," "discord," "difference," "misunderstanding," "wrangling," and so on. For many of us, "conflict" means "anger," "aggressiveness," "hostility"—nothing to suggest that conflict has a positive side. Yet conflict is an inevitable and necessary part of human experience, and that applies to conflicts within ourselves about our personal needs and development as well as the conflicts that occur in relationships with others. In this chapter we will deal with the latter.

Many conflicts exist in relationships, and in E.T.W. we categorize them in two groups: those that erupt when *needs* are interfered with—conflict of needs—and those that start because of a difference in *values* between people—values collisions. (We deal with ways to handle the latter type in Chapter XI.)

In a conflict of needs, each party can clearly understand and accept that the other has unmet needs and that these needs are important and valid. Obviously, the more tangible the needs are, the more likely the other person will accept their validity.

Here are some examples of conflict-of-needs situations:

You have one television set. Your son and you continually differ about which show to watch.

You and one of your subordinates both need the company conference room for meetings at the same time.

You and your spouse have a small amount of savings. He wants to buy a new car; you want to invest it in real estate.

Your daughter and you both want to use the family car on the same night.

You want to have a baby in the near future; you husband wants to wait a few years.

Your coworker smokes constantly in the office you share. The smoke makes you cough and sneeze.

Your boyfriend wants to get married; you want to continue living together unmarried.

You're divorced and have two children. Your ex-husband is refusing to continue paying child support.

Take a few minutes to identify and list some real conflict-of-needs situations in your own life.

In our E.T.W. classes we teach a specific method that will greatly increase your effectiveness in resolving conflicts like these. But first it's important to understand why we fear conflicts in our relationships, and to be aware of how we typically try to resolve them.

WHY WE TRY TO AVOID CONFLICT

Why are conflicts frightening to so many people? It's probably accurate to say that situations in our lives involving conflict with others cause more fear and stress than any other kind. We don't know the outcome. We don't want to lose. We're afraid we won't be able to control ourselves. We fear the relationship will suffer.

For women, the issue of conflict is especially critical. Most of us have learned that conflict, like anger and anxiety, is to be denied, avoided, unexpressed. We have all heard people say things such as:

"We never fight."

"I'll do anything to keep peace in the family."

"In all the years we've been married we've never had a serious disagreement."

These people are saying, in effect, that their conflicts are not open, not out on the table. They have chosen either not to recognize their conflicts or to deal with them in indirect ways. In fact, much anger and anxiety in relationships results from failure to face conflicts openly and directly. Therefore, they continue to be unresolved, or are resolved in unsatisfactory ways.

Many women have had painful experiences with conflict at various times in their lives. A woman commenting on her fear of conflict traces it to:

"Those scenes between my parents. They would erupt anytime, anywhere, without warning. I can remember lying in bed, upstairs, hearing their voices growing louder and louder, and I would bury my head in the pillow so I wouldn't hear."

Think back about your early experiences with conflict. Consider how your own parents handled conflicts between themselves and with you.

As women we also learned to assume responsibility for being peacemakers, for making sure everyone else is happy. We often intervene in conflicts between other people so no one feels hurt or upset, as reported by E.T.W. participants:

"When my husband gets angry at one of the kids, I immediately jump in and defend the kid, or try to solve the problem myself. Then my husband gets mad at *me!*"

"I noticed recently how I forget what I want to say, and I automatically become the peacemaker in our business meetings when other people start arguing."

The main reason people, especially women, try to avoid engaging in open conflict is that past conflicts so often were resolved in inequitable ways. Instead of being recognized as evidence of unmet needs, these conflicts become power struggles. Eventually there is a winner and a loser. And since most of us naturally want our relationships to feel fair and reciprocal, power struggles can be a way of trying to restore balance in a relationship. However, power struggles inevitably result in one or both persons feeling like a loser because they don't get their needs met.

Let's take a closer look at power and at the typical win-lose methods used for resolving conflicts in relationships before describing our nonpower No-lose Method.

USING POWER TO RESOLVE CONFLICTS

We define "power" here as one person's control over the resources another needs, and the willingness to use (or threaten to use) that control to get others to do something she or he would not otherwise do, or to do something she or he does not want to do.*

Resources are what we all need to survive—to make our lives satisfying and productive. They include such concrete things as money (and what it buys), sex, food, shelter, information; and also such intangibles as love, approval, recognition, affirmation.

When people have the resources to satisfy the needs of another, they're in a position to decide whether to give them or withhold them. They can decide to re-

*It is to be distinguished from the positive connotation of personal power—strength, capacity, and courage to control your life and fulfill your needs in a self-directing way.

ward or punish the other person's behavior. Punishment, in addition to withholding of rewards, includes the capacity to cause physical or emotional pain—spanking a child or firing an employee. The threat of using punitive power to control another's behavior can be just as effective (and destructive to the relationship) as its actual use.

This kind of power works best when one person is far more dependent on the other to satisfy her or his needs. For example:

Young children are almost totally dependent on their parents for survival.

An employee who has a fairly unmarketable skill is very dependent on hor or hio present employer.

A wife who doesn't earn money—or have access to it—is dependent on her husband.

When relationships are more interdependent—i.e., what I need from you and what you need from me are more or less equal—coercive power is much less likely to work.

Coercive power can be used directly or indirectly. Although we tend to think of power in its more blatant, obvious forms, there are many subtle, manipulative, indirect ways to use power, often as a defense against the direct use of power by another. Powerless people who don't have *as much* access to the resources, people who have learned to avoid conflict, or people who fear open conflict tend to resort to indirect or subtle power.

Many women, especially, view themselves as persons who don't use power in their relationships, when in fact they are just not using it directly or openly. Here are some examples of the use of indirect power:

A wife getting a headache at bedtime

One spouse refusing to talk to the other

A wife starting to cry when her husband wants to talk

One spouse getting sick just before an important trip they were planning to take

An employee "forgetting" to get important work out

Whether power is used directly or indirectly, almost all of us are in positions where others can use power over us, and also in positions where we can use power over others. The head nurse in a large metropolitan hospital reports:

"At work I feel powerful in relation to the patients as well as the nurses I supervise, and when any of them act up, I don't hesitate to show them who's boss. But at home, my husband runs the show, and I find myself submitting to his wishes in order to avoid arguments."

A power differential of some size exists in most relationships between people—one person has the power to get her or his needs met at the expense of the other. If that person *uses* the power in a conflict situation, one person usually wins, the other loses. The loser then feels motivated to win at the other's expense in the next conflict. It becomes a vicious cycle; the result can be a gradual erosion of the relationship.

When men and women discuss their relations with each other, they often say that the two forms of power used most frequently are money and sex. A man in his mid-forties, a television writer, tells a marriage counselor:

"I gave my wife everything . . . a beautiful home, a car of her own, whatever she wanted. And then, all of a sudden, she wants to go back to school to get a college degree. She is almost forty, can you believe it? I refused to pay the tuition fees. I figured I had to do something to keep her from making a fool of herself. So she up and gets herself a job and she's going to college at night. And where does that leave me? I feel as though I don't have much of a home or marriage anymore. I don't understand it. I've always given her everything."

A woman whose husband is a vice-president of a large company tells us:

"My husband started moving up the career ladder, and soon he was working late evenings or bringing work home. It made me feel neglected and pushed aside. He was so proud of the way I looked—I used to be a model—so I started neglecting my appearance and putting on weight. And when he'd come to bed, I'd pretend to be fast asleep. Of course, I was doing all these things to punish him. We're working things out now, but I can tell you we had some very rough years."

TYPICAL WAYS OF RESOLVING CONFLICTS

In E.T.W. these win-lose methods of resolving con flicts are called Method I and Method II. Both are power-based methods; both have a win-lose orientation—there is always a winner and a loser. Neither method allows hidden conflict to surface in positive, constructive ways. Although people normally have a propensity toward one method or the other, invariably they use both. Let's discuss each in greater detail.

Method I—You Win, Other Loses

In this situation, you make use of your power in the relationship to get your needs met at the expense of the other. You get your way. Your solution prevails. As a result, you get resentment from the other person, as illustrated (the pluses and minuses in the diagram stand for possession of rewards and punishments):

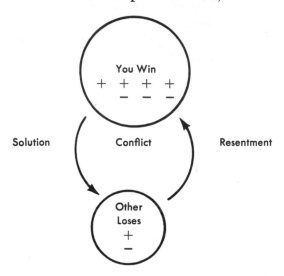

When you use Method I to resolve conflicts, the others' reactions to you are quite predictable (Method I has many of the same characteristics of aggressive behavior described in Chapter III). Since others are left with unmet needs—and a feeling that problems and conflicts are solved unfairly—you often get such reactions as:

They start fearing you.

They criticize you, talk about you behind your back.

They try to sabotage your efforts to meet your other needs.

They form alliances to counteract your power.

They start disliking you, avoiding you when possible.

They lie to you.

They often don't express their true feelings when you're around, but tell you what you want to hear.

They often covertly meet their needs, disregard your orders.

They try to win your favor, usually through manipulation.

They stop communicating their important needs to you.

Getting your needs met at the expense of others damages relationships, because the others will grow increasingly resentful toward you. They also will be reluctant to engage in open conflict with you, because they know you're inclined to use your power to win. Since conflicts don't really get resolved satisfactorily, they keep coming up again and again in various ways, because the other person didn't get her or his needs met.

Here are some examples of Method I:

1. One of your subordinates would like to have a promotion. You refuse to consider it.

2. Your son wants very badly to take a weekend trip with his friends. You refuse to allow him to go.

Using power on people has often been defended because it presumably assures "survival of the fittest." The general idea behind this proposition is that nature intended the strong to dominate the weak. Nature, like God and Fate, is often called on to justify self-interested behavior, yet there is no evidence, scientific or otherwise, that in human relationships the cosmic scheme calls for domination of the weak by the strong. On the contrary, there is ample evidence that in personal relationships the use of superior strength or power usually has negative effects on all parties concerned.

Marriage counselors tell us that few marriages can withstand the strain of one partner dominating the other for any length of time. Sooner or later, a "volcano effect" will erupt from the accumulated resentment of the partner who has been kept in a weakened position. Or there may be a quiet and steady withdrawal until the subordinated person is no longer really "there." She or he will make an outward show of compliance ("Yes, dear, whatever you say"), but all the vital signs, the marks of a distinctive personality, have gone underground.

IDENTIFYING THE EFFECTS OF POWER

Take a few minutes to recall some of the effects power has had on your own life. Ask yourself:

What kinds of power have other people used on me? Still use on me?

My boss?

My spouse?

My children?

My friends?

My parents?

How do I feel toward people who use power over me?

What kinds of power have I used most frequently in my relationships with others? Still use?

What are my feelings about myself when I use power?

Method II—You Lose, Other Wins

In this conflict situation, you have most of the power (or it's equal) and you allow the other to meet her or his needs at your expense. You give in. The other person's solution prevails. Now you have feelings of resentment toward the other person, as shown here:

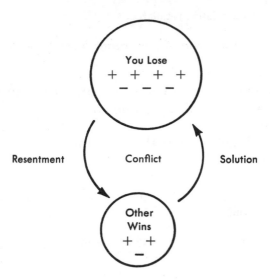

Method II is most commonly used by people who want to avoid conflict; they want peace at any price. The problem is, they pay a very high price for this peace. Unlike Method I, the consequences of Method II are *your* negative feelings (much the same as the nonassertive behavior described in Chapter III). Since you don't get your needs met, you may experience many of these reactions:

You feel resentful and angry toward others.

You sabotage their efforts to meet their other needs.

You gradually withdraw from such relationships.

You feel a sense of frustration and anxiety because of unmet needs.

You avoid future conflicts.

You start feeling indifferent, apathetic, depressed.

You often covertly meet your needs in other ways.

You decide to win later, retaliate.

You lose respect for yourself, have decreasing self-esteem; others lose respect for you, also.

Again, since your needs are not met, the conflict is still unresolved, and will continue to exist and come up in various ways.

Here is how Method II works in the two cases mentioned earlier:

1. Although you don't feel your employee merits a promotion, you give her one.

2. You give in to your son's arguments and allow him to go with his friends.

NO-LOSE CONFLICT RESOLUTION—METHOD III

In E.T.W. we teach an alternative to the two win-lose methods of resolving conflicts. It is based on nonuse of power. The idea is that conflicts in relationships can be dealt with openly and honestly; that both people can get their needs met; that neither has to lose. We call this the No-lose Method, Method III. It is a way to achieve mutual need satisfaction.

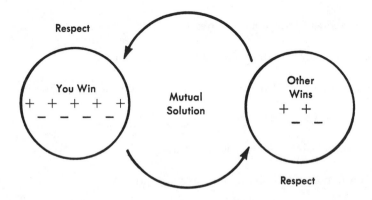

Method III requires a commitment from both people not to use power to meet their own needs at the other's expense. Because most of us have learned to resolve conflicts in win-lose ways, this adjustment is not easy to make. It can be especially difficult for people who possess a large degree of power in most of their relationships.

When we can get the courage to make such a commitment to others with whom we have close relationships, the outcome can be very gratifying. Some benefits of applying this No-lose Method are:

1. Allows conflict to surface, be expressed and resolved in constructive, fair ways.

2. People learn that conflict can produce exciting, interesting changes; they start seeing it positively, start initiating it, stop avoiding it.

3. Each person takes personal responsibility for getting her or his needs met, and not at the expense of the other. (Unwillingness to lose is a key element.)

4. People are far more likely to deal with basic, real conflicts, not superficial ones.

5. The same conflict doesn't keep coming up over and over again because it was resolved fairly.

6. Better solutions to conflicts are generated when all involved participate; get the benefit of each person's creative thinking.

7. Both people are far more committed to carrying out the decision when they participate in making it, rather than having it imposed on them.

8. People feel closer and more loving toward each other—resentment and hostility dissipate.

9. Others start seeing this as a model for solving conflicts in other relationships as well.

Using our examples, here are *possible* Method III solutions (there could be many others) to the problems:

1. You and your employee have a conference. Each of you states feelings and needs and listens to the other. After a full discussion, you *mutually* agree that a promotion at present is premature; *together*, you set goals for the employee and agree to meet again in six months to reconsider the promotion.

2. You and your son sit down and share feelings and needs and listen to each other. The two of you make an agreement that he can go if a parent or older brother or sister goes along.

LOOKING AT CONFLICT POSITIVELY

If we can start looking at the existence of conflict as evidence of unmet needs (instead of a struggle to get the upper hand), we can see it in an entirely new way. Conflict can be healthy. It can be a positive force in our lives. It can act as an invitation to congruent communication, offering an opportunity to engage in open, honest confrontation. It can clear the air and, by dissolving misunderstanding, bring people closer to each other.

People expand and develop through the process of initiating and engaging in conflict. In fact, disagreements are probably far more helpful than agreements for stimulating healthy change and growth in relationships. Without conflict there would be no change and little progress. Life would be bland, boring, and static.

Just as anger and anxiety can be accepted as valid, conflict, too, can be viewed more positively. Just as the individual can grow and develop by effectively overcoming anxiety, relationships can grow through the effective resolution of conflicts. Therefore, it is important to learn effective ways of settling conflicts in relationships.

X. NO-LOSE CONFLICT RESOLUTION

*You and I have a conflict of needs. I respect your needs,
but I must respect my own, too. I will not use my power
over you so I win and you lose, but I cannot give in and
let you win at the expense of my losing. So let's agree to
search together for a solution that would satisfy your
needs and also satisfy mine, so no one loses.*

THOMAS GORDON

No-lose conflict resolution works if you go
through these six steps:

I.   Defining the problem

II. Generating possible solutions

III. Evaluating solutions

IV. Deciding on a mutually acceptable solution

V.   Acting on the solution

VI. Checking the results of the solution

SETTING THE STAGE FOR USING METHOD III

Before describing these steps and demonstrating
how Method III can work in actual situations, here are
some preliminary guidelines to keep in mind.

1. Each person must make a commitment not to use her or his power
   in finding a solution to the conflict.

Be realistic about the relationships in which you can freely use Method III. Obviously, in many of your relationships where another person has power over you, it's probably going to be difficult, perhaps impossible.

You can put Method III to work most easily and successfully when you hold power over the other person or when the power is fairly equal. Some examples of relationships in which you usually hold the power are:

You	*Other*
Parent	Child
Boss	Subordinate
Teacher	Student

Some examples where power might be fairly equal are:

You	*Other*
Friend	Friend
Relative	Relative
Wife	Husband

Relationships where Method III might not work because the other person has power over you and is not willing to solve problems without it are:

You	*Other*
Subordinate	Boss
Student	Teacher
Wife	Husband

Many women find themselves in the relationships where the other person has power and uses it to get her or his own way.

Is there anything you can do in lieu of continuing to lose —short of ending the relationship? While some people are adamantly opposed to not using their power, many others solve problems with power out of habit and/or because they don't know any other way except giving in—and they don't like that alternative.

To influence the other person to enter into Method III conflict resolution with you, you need to take the initiative:

Send Preventive I-Messages such as:

"I'd like to see if there's another way to solve this problem. What would you think of our sitting down together and trying to find a solution that we would both like?"

"I'm really excited about some ideas I'm learning in that class I'm taking. I'd like to try to use them in our relationship. Would you be willing?"

"I value our relationship so much that I'd really like to try some new ways of solving our problems. I'd like to tell you about them."

Send strong Confrontive I-Messages about how you feel about losing and/or how you feel about the other person when she or he continually wins at your expense:

"I feel so hurt and frustrated when you make decisions without including me, because often it means I don't get what I need. It makes me feel you don't care what I want."

"I feel myself getting really resentful because you change the subject when I tell you my ideas about the budget. I'm afraid some things that are important to me will be left out."

"I don't feel very loving toward you when we always do things your way. It makes me feel like trying to get back at you."

If you can express your feelings in self-disclosing, non-threatening ways and shift gears to listen to any resistance, you may be surprised at the positive response you get from others.

2. After agreeing to try Method III, each person must clearly understand that each of you will search for a solution in which neither will lose. Knowing the six steps is also essential. You can tell the other person what they are or let her or him read about them.

3. Choose a time when you can be free from distractions. Method III can be time-consuming because it's open-ended. In your family, Sunday afternoon might be a good time. In your office, you might suggest a meeting a week in advance to fit the schedules of those involved. With a friend, it might be the next time you have lunch.

4. Be sure to record suggested solutions to the problem. For a group, this could be on a blackboard or a chart pad. Paper and pencil may be sufficient for two people.

THE SIX STEPS OF NO-LOSE PROBLEM SOLVING

Step I: Defining the Problem—in Terms of Needs, Not Competing Solutions

This is by far the most critical step (and often the most time-consuming) in problem-solving. A clear sense of each other's needs is essential for moving toward a solution to meet those needs. The most effective way to state the problem is in direct, honest, self-disclosing I-Messages. Your statement of the problem should not communicate blame or judgment of the other person.

In this first step you're concerned with *needs,* not yet with *solutions.* Learning to distinguish needs from solutions may take some practice, especially since most of us are inclined to express our solutions to our needs rather than our needs themselves. We leap to solutions before thoroughly exploring the needs. Often there can be many possible solutions to a particular need. Some pretty obvious examples of needs and solutions are:

Needs	*Possible Solutions*
Transportation	Ride your bicycle. Ask a friend for a ride. Borrow a car. Take a bus.
More free time	Divide up household chores among family. Hire outside help. Quit full-time job, get part-time job. Get up earlier.
More exercise	Join exercise class. Learn to play tennis. Start jogging. Do more housework.
Desire to have fun	Go out with friends. Have a party. Plan a weekend outing. Play a game.
More storage space	Have a garage sale. Rent storage space. Give unused items away. Build a storage room.
Mental stimulation	Take a college course. Read more interesting books. Attend lectures and debates. Subscribe to interesting magazines and journals.

A cautionary note: someone may start out with one problem and, after being listened to by the other person, discover she or he is really talking about a different or deeper problem.

Take enough time to define the problem or conflict accurately. Be willing to shift gears back and forth from sending I-Messages to Active Listening.

Before moving to Step II, be certain that both of you agree about the definition of the problem(s). Often (especially when you have not used a no-lose method of conflict resolution before), it becomes clear through disclosing and listening that *more* than one conflict exists between you and the other person. It might be helpful to list each of them; decide which have the highest priority; and work them out one at a time.

Step II: Generating Possible Solutions (Brainstorming)

This is the creative part of the problem-solving, the stage when both of you are saying: "Let's put our heads together and find a constructive solution." It's often difficult to think of a good solution immediately; still, initial solutions, though often not acceptable in themselves, tend to trigger ideas that lead to better ones. You might want to ask the other party for possible solutions before offering yours.

To make the most of this stage, it's best if both of you:

See this as a truly creative experience, and feel free to express all ideas you have for solutions.

Use Active Listening to clarify or make certain you understand all solutions, and write them down, if possible.

Avoid judging or criticizing the other's solutions.

Try to list a lot of possible solutions before evaluating or discussing any particular one. Remember, you're trying to arrive at the *best*—not just any—solution.

If the process falters, restate the problem in terms of *needs*. Sometimes this starts the wheels turning again.

When you've exhausted your creative thinking, and have a list of possible solutions, you're ready to go on to the next step.

Step III: Evaluating Solutions

Now both of you will want to do a lot of critical thinking. What are the flaws, if any, in the suggested solutions? Are they fair to both? Does one solution seem more workable than the others? Any reason why it might not work? Will it be too difficult to put into action?

Eliminate solutions that both agree will not meet the mutual needs.

Sometimes while you're evaluating solutions, a brand-new one will emerge, better than any of the others; or an earlier one will be improved by some modification that now suggests itself. If you fail to test your solutions at this stage, you'll naturally increase the chance of ending up with a poor solution or one that will not be carried out seriously.

Step IV: Deciding on a Mutually Acceptable Solution

Now a commitment to a mutually acceptable solution can be made. Usually, when all facts are exposed and several possibilities have been weighed and analyzed, you'll find yourself closing in on a solution that satisfies both your needs. Often it'll be a combination of two or more of the suggested ideas. Don't try to persuade (or push a solution on) the other person, and don't be persuaded by the other to buy a solution you don't like. If both people don't freely choose a solution, chances are it will not be carried out.

When you appear to be close to an outcome acceptable to both, state the solution to make certain both of you understand it. When you do, you may want to put it in writing to be sure that future misunderstandings can be checked against the decision you've both agreed on.

Step V: Acting on the Solution

Because it's one thing to create a solution and another thing to carry it out, discuss your plan for action immediately after your agreement has been reached. Decide who is to do what by which date. It's constructive to assume that the other will carry out the decision; therefore, do not raise the question of consequences if it isn't done. In most situations, the correlation between mutual confidence and effective performance is high.

Avoid pressuring the other person to carry out the assigned tasks through such statements as:

"Now, I hope you plan to stick to this agreement!"

"You know, making this agreement means you promise to do your part."

An important assumption of the No-lose Method is that the participants are responsible and trustworthy; that, given support and understanding, they'll carry out their obligations. Monitoring and nagging tend to foster dependency and resentment rather than individual responsibility.

However, because many people are unaccustomed to Method III problem-solving, initially they may not assume responsibility for carrying out solutions. If, as time passes, the other party to the decision fails to carry out her or his part of the agreement, you'll need to reopen your discussion with a confrontive I-Message such as:

"I'm really disappointed and upset because we made an agreement about this conflict and you haven't stuck to it!"

The other person then realizes that you expect her or him to be responsible.

When the No-lose philosophy becomes more natural to you and the people in your life, you will find that solutions can be reached and put into action with a minimum of delays and difficulties.

Step VI: Checking the Results of the Solution

Now it's time to evaluate the effectiveness of your solution by asking yourself: is it in fact meeting both our needs?

Since so many unpredictable elements complicate the problems and conflicts that people encounter in their lives, your Method III problem-solving will not always produce the most satisfactory result. Maybe, in achieving one goal you endanger another, more important one. Or, in time, circumstances change so drastically that your original solution no longer works. Or you may discover weaknesses in the solution that require modification.

Sometimes people new to Method III find they over-committed themselves; in letting their enthusiasm carry them away, they agreed to do the impossible. Be sure to keep the door open for revisions if this happens. To prevent it from happening in the first place, try to be realistic about your solution as well as what it will take to put it into operation.

Remember, you're engaged in an ongoing, open-ended process. Your self-disclosure and listening skills are being constantly sharpened and refined. As you get more practice and success in using Method III, it will become easier to regard conflicts as evidence of unmet needs, which offer ways for relationships to grow and develop in new and exciting directions.

USING METHOD III TO SOLVE A CONFLICT
IN THE FAMILY

To show how Method III can work, here is an example from a family genuinely committed to the No-lose philosophy.

As frequently happens, this conflict became apparent when the woman, Bonnie, sent a Confrontive I-Message to her husband, Jim, and her 11-year-old daughter, Sunny, describing her feelings and problem about the housework. She recalls:

"I started working full-time about a year ago. Before that, I'd taken almost total responsibility for the household. A couple of months after I started working, I began to start feeling kind of resentful toward Jim and Sunny. Not only was I working full-time, but I was also still doing most of the housework. I guess I'd expected they would automatically start helping, and when they didn't I must admit I said such things as: 'Could you help me with some of this work?' 'Can't you see all the things that need to be done?' 'I'm just going to stop doing any work around here.' 'How can you sit there and watch television while I do all the work?'

"Then they'd get up and do a few things—or we would argue —and the problem would come up again a day or so later. I decided this was a very important issue for me—and I was unwilling to keep losing. Even after some pretty good Confrontive I-Messages, I didn't get much response."

Defining the Problem

After a *series* of increasingly strong Confrontive I-Messages, the three of them agreed there was a problem and sat down to discuss it. To define it, each discussed her or his feelings about housework. They agreed that none liked to do it, especially the routine, daily chores. Some of the expressed needs and feelings were:

Bonnie's Needs	*Jim's Needs*	*Sunny's Needs*
Need for fairly clean house	Bonnie's standards too high	Some need for clean house
Not to do so much of the work herself	Need for reasonably clean house	Need to be cooperative
Overloaded with responsibility	Need to be cooperative	Need not to be hassled
Need to feel less pressure	Need for time to relax	Need for time to watch TV, be with friends

After much discussion, Bonnie, Jim, and Sunny decided that the daily jobs of cooking dinner, doing dishes afterward, picking up around the house, and doing grocery shopping were the main responsibilities. Some jobs were already being done by each person (such as making own breakfast, making and changing own bed, paying bills), and that arrangement was satisfactory to everyone. Further discussion about the other jobs brought out:

Possible Solutions

1. Bonnie could lower her standards about housework.

2. One person could cook, another clean up.

3. Take turns cooking and cleaning up.

4. Choose favorite job and do that.

5. Each be responsible for own cooking, laundry, etc.

6. Everyone pick up after herself or himself.

7. Hire outside help.

Evaluating Solutions

1. Agreed it was impractical for each to do all her or his own work.

2. Decided that outside help would be good for weekly jobs, but it wouldn't solve daily problems.

Deciding on a Mutually Acceptable Solution

1. Each agreed to clean up own breakfast dishes and put food and newspapers away every morning.

2. Each agreed to pick up her or his own shoes, magazines, dishes, etc., and put them away before going to bed each night.

3. Each agreed to be responsible for cooking dinner and washing the dishes two nights a week. (They usually went out on Friday or Saturday night.)

4. Bonnie and Jim agreed to do grocery shopping together, or take turns.

5. Sunny agreed to put groceries away.

6. Bonnie and Jim agreed the last person up makes their bed.

Acting on the Solution

All agreed to start right away.

Checking the Results of the Solution

After a couple of months of trying this plan, Bonnie realized that much of the housework that she did still was not included, and she asked for another problem-solving meeting to revise the original plan. She stated her needs to Jim and Sunny. All agreed that the problem was to figure out new ways to get all the housework done. They decided to start by listing all the jobs to be done (Jim and

Sunny didn't realize how many were being done by Bonnie). Possible solutions were:

1. Divide work equally among all three.

2. Hire a housekeeper for a few hours a week.

3. Every person responsible for all own needs, i.e., cooking, laundry, etc.

4. Each pick favorite jobs, do those.

Evaluating Solutions

Bonnie, Jim, and Sunny again eliminated the idea of each being responsible for all of her or his own needs; it was impractical, and they had a need for this to be a cooperative effort.

They discussed the pros and cons of Bonnie's standards. Bonnie felt it wasn't that they were so high; the problem was that Jim and Sunny were accustomed to having the house reasonably clean, and were not aware of how much time and energy Bonnie spent to keep it that way.

They discussed their values about housework—how it's been "woman's work," the issues of traditional sex roles, how Bonnie's and Jim's parents had handled housework, its degree of importance to each of them, the need to have time to relax, the need to be cooperative and fair.

Deciding on a Mutually Acceptable Solution

After lots of discussion, Bonnie, Jim, and Sunny decided on a combination of dividing work equally among all three, and hiring someone for five or six hours a week. They started by revising their original plan, and agreed each person would be responsible for cooking dinner, cleaning up dishes and kitchen, and sweeping family room and kitchen two nights a week. (The rest of their original agreement remained the same.) In addition, each agreed to do the following:

Bonnie Agreed to Do	Jim Agreed to Do	Sunny Agreed to Do
All laundry for Jim and herself and general laundry, folding, putting clothes away	All grocery shopping, making list, putting food away	All dusting of wooden furniture in house
Taking all trash out on Sunday night	Taking and picking up of dry cleaning	Watering some outdoor plants
Watering and fertilizing all indoor plants	Calling repair people for household needs and arranging to meet them	Her own laundry
Shaking throw rugs and sweeping hallway and porch	Taking cars for repair, maintenance	Cleaning her own room

They agreed that the person they would hire for five or six hours a week would vacuum, clean bathrooms, change sheets, etc. Additional agreements were that they would work together when they invited guests for dinner; share shopping for Christmas presents; share jobs like cleaning the garage. The most available parent would take Sunny to dental appointments, friends' homes, etc. They decided to implement the plan immediately.

Checking the Results

The family members commented:

Bonnie: Each of us often helps the other; we feel closer. We all feel more responsible now. I feel greatly relieved, feel less pressure, and have much less resentment.

Although we still have problems about housework and probably always will, I feel we have made a very significant advance in the way we live. The most important reason we were able to reach this agreement was a growing awareness by Jim (and Sunny to a lesser extent) and a gradual change in attitude about this problem. I continued to confront this problem over quite a long time; many times it was painful and difficult, and it still is at times. But housework is no longer regarded as "woman's work" in our family.

Jim: Working through this problem made me realize just how many jobs were required in our household, and I was surprised how many of these were done by Bonnie. While I certainly wasn't overjoyed about taking on some of these jobs, I couldn't deny that a better distribution would be a lot fairer. I find it hard to remember everything I agreed to do, because for such a long time these things were done for me. But it gets easier every day. Frankly, I feel a lot better about myself now—none of the old guilt I used to have. Best of all, Bonnie is happier and more loving to me and Sunny. One unexpected outcome: for some reason Sunny has decided to go with me and help me when I shop for food each week. I like these times together with her—just the two of us.

Sunny: It's working out pretty good. We always seemed to be fighting before. But lots of times I don't remember to get stuff out of the freezer. When I have time and I'm bored I like to do housework. I think it's fair—because we [Jim and Sunny] never did anything before.

PROBLEM-SOLVING IN A GROUP MEETING

Most of us divide our lives between two-way relationships and participation in group activities, at work or elsewhere, so we need problem-solving tools for group as well as individual situations. The tools are similar in many ways, but important differences exist.

The group process has a big advantage over one-to-one problem-solving: it provides support for an individual—you're usually not alone with the conflict. The disadvantage is that you might be reluctant to expose before a group feelings that you would be willing to share with one other person. Some nonassertive people find groups especially inhibiting; they tend to go along with whatever they perceive to be the will of the majority—or of the group leader, especially if she or he is regarded as a powerful person. (One of the most serious mistakes a group leader can make is to try to force nonassertive members to participate. This will only raise their level of anxiety and make it more difficult for them to develop a sense of personal responsibility—the prerequisite for free and active participation.)

A few additional guidelines for group problem-solving:

Include only people who are involved in the problem.

Make certain that the problem is within a particular group's "area of freedom" to solve; that is, the group has the freedom to consider, select, and act on the solution to the problem.

Be sure each person understands how Method III works.

Set aside adequate time to be free from distractions.

Don't vote as a last attempt to settle the problem. (Voting is win-lose.) Every group member must be willing to *accept* the solution, though not necessarily completely agree with it.

AN EXAMPLE OF GROUP PROBLEM-SOLVING

Here's an account of an unplanned problem-solving experience with Method III at an E.T.W. Instructor Training Workshop. The group consisted of fifteen participants, plus the instructor trainer. The location was an air-conditioned hotel conference room. Four participants were smokers, the rest nonsmokers. When the problem came up, the group had been meeting for two days and was almost halfway through the course. The conflict was initiated by a nonsmoking member. Her Confrontive I-Message:

"I've been uncomfortable since the beginning of the workshop because of the smoke in this room. My eyes are red and irritated, my head feels dizzy. I'm having trouble concentrating, and it's interfering with my participation in the course."

Then other nonsmokers also began to express their discomfort. The instructor saw the existence of a group problem. Even though the class had not yet reached the session on Method III, she explained briefly how this conflict of needs could be solved by the group to meet both sets of needs. She then Active Listened to help the group define the problem in terms of the needs on each side, and helped the class go through the six steps.

The problem was defined this way:

Smokers' Needs	*Nonsmokers' Needs*
Physical need for cigarettes at regular intervals	Physical need to be comfortable, and not breathe smoke
Need to be present at all times in order not to miss anything during a smoking break	Desire to keep group together
Need to feel part of the group, not isolated	Need to respect rights and needs of the smokers
Need not to impose on others.	Need not to hurt smokers' feelings

Going on to Step II, the brainstorming stage, they came up with the following suggested solutions:

1. Set up smoking-nonsmoking sections in the room

2. Establish a no-smoking rule

3. Provide frequent smoke breaks

4. Nonsmokers wear gas masks

5. Have a fan brought into room to circulate air

6. Permit smoking only outside the room

7. Permit smoking only at the door, with door kept partially open to let smoke escape

8. Permit smoking during half of each session, no smoking for the remaining half

9. Conduct an air-current experiment to determine direction in which smoke travels; arrange smokers and nonsmokers accordingly

10. Have only one person smoke at a time

11. Move to an adequately ventilated room

Evaluating the suggested solutions (Step III), the group began eliminating those that could not be implemented or did not satisfy both sets of needs. The proposals that survived were numbers 7, 9, and 10. The group discussed the pros and cons of these three proposed solutions, and discussed how they might work.

This yielded the suggestions that smokers be grouped near the door, with the door kept partially open, and smoking be permitted one at a time only.

Now the group was ready for Step IV: deciding on a

mutually acceptable solution. The discussion that followed was directed toward a formula that would combine the three agreed-on solutions. The result was: the air-current experiment showed the section of the room toward which the smoke traveled. Seating was rearranged so nonsmokers were placed in the smoke-free section, smokers on the other side of the room. Smokers agreed to smoke one at a time, sitting near the exit door with the door kept partially open during cigarette breaks, so much of the smoke would flow toward the outside.

The plan was put into action at once (Step V), and evaluated (Step VI) from time to time. The two sides agreed it was working well and both sets of needs had been met.

Follow-up

In a short discussion following this 45-minute problem-solving process, participants reported the following feelings and insights:

This was the first time many had participated in this kind of problem-solving, particularly in a large group; some had expressed doubt that this problem could be solved fairly; they felt really good about its success.

Sharing honest negative feelings was difficult for some; nonsmokers were afraid of hurting smokers' feelings.

Feelings of anxiety decreased as each saw others' willingness to be self-disclosing and cooperative; trust developed.

Each "side" developed respect for the needs of the other.

When the conflict was resolved, participants felt closer to each other.

Participants expressed appreciation for the instructor's effectiveness in guiding them through this process.

They were then able to continue work in a new spirit of cooperation.

Whether you're involved in either a two-way or a group conflict, remember that your most effective tools for problem-solving are:

Clear and honest disclosure of your feelings and needs

Active Listening to feelings and needs of the other

Trust and respect for the needs of the other

Openness to changing facts and feelings

Entering into Method III without fixed solutions

Refusal to revert to Methods I and II

An unwillingness to let Method III fail

XI. RESOLVING VALUES COLLISIONS

If we are to achieve a richer culture, rich in contrasting
values, we must recognize the whole gamut of human
potentialities, and so weave a less arbitrary social fabric,
one in which each diverse human gift will find a fitting
place.

MARGARET MEAD

CONSIDER these situations:

Your husband refuses to go to church with you.

Your child uses language you don't approve of.

Your daughter decides to quit college and join a dance group, against
your advice.

Your friend takes a "personal growth" course whose philosophy you
feel is dangerous.

Ask yourself the following questions about these potential conflict situations:

How is the other person's behavior actually preventing me from meeting my needs?

Is there a *tangible* effect of the other's behavior on me?

Does the other person believe that this behavior *tangibly* affects me?

Now recall some conflicts you've recognized in your
own relationships when you could *not* describe a tangible
effect of the other's behavior on you.

141

You've seen how effectively the No-lose Method can work in conflict-of-needs situations. You'll recall how, in the smoking/no-smoking controversy, by concentrating on mutual needs and tangible effects, the involved people moved toward a resolution satisfactory to both sides.

When our mutual needs are in conflict, we *can* negotiate, adapt, compromise, so neither loses. We're usually willing to change behavior or try to find a mutually acceptable solution when we understand that our behavior is having an undesirable effect, in some tangible way, on people who are important in our lives. But when a difference in deeply felt *values* is central to the conflict, the situation changes. Our resistance stiffens when we feel that our behavior has no *readily* discernible or tangible effect on the other person. We call such situations "values collisions."

WHAT IS A VALUES COLLISION?

In a values collision, you and another person strongly disagree on a certain issue, yet neither of you is tangibly affected by the difference. (Recall that we defined tangible effects as those that cost you time, money, energy.)

Most values collisions emerge from deeply held beliefs, opinions, or personal tastes, and many don't lend themselves to Method III problem-solving. People who are willing to negotiate about needs—storage space at home, perhaps, or a quiet place to study, or an adjusted work schedule—may see no reason why they should problem-solve on such issues of values as lifestyles, morals, religious or political beliefs, personal tastes, or goals. "What I think or believe is my business" would sum up their attitude.

Here's how a values collision shows up on the Behavior Rectangle (note how the No-Problem Area becomes continually enlarged):

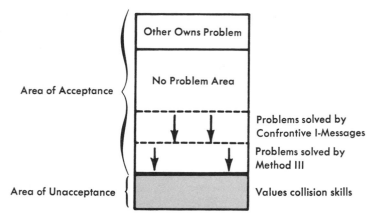

Like other kinds of conflicts, values collisions are inevitable in human relationships, because we constantly come into contact with people whose view of the world is very different from our own. In our kind of society there is no one set of approved values. We bring to our relationships the beliefs and attitudes that come out of our widely varying backgrounds and experience. If we want to expand our horizons and enrich our lives, we need to be able to make connections with people whose values may at times come into direct conflict with ours.

Of course, a values collision, though normal, can be frustrating and painful, particularly in relationships that are important to you.

Statements such as these are signs that values conflicts are unresolved in these relationships:

"I can't get along with my husband's family. They have very different ideas about how we should bring up our children."

"My career is in trouble because my boss and I don't agree about personnel policies."

"I'm afraid to say what I really think because my ideas are considered far out and people withdraw from me."

The issue of values and values collisions can be especially painful for women. Many women have been encouraged or forced to adopt values (or at least live in accordance with values) not their own because others have had power over them. This is true for several reasons. Among them are:

Women's financial dependence on men, at home and at work

A desire to get along, keep the peace, avoid arguing and fighting

A lack of trust in their own perceptions, ideas, opinions, and values

As a result, you might find yourself:

Switching to your husband's religion or political party

Finally agreeing to move to a new area that your husband likes, but you don't

Reluctantly going on a camping trip

Having people for dinner whom you don't particularly like

Going out with your company's clients, or behaving seductively at office parties

And since women have for so long been encouraged to conciliate, be agreeable, and not trust their own perceptions of reality, they have often felt more threatened by conflicts involving values than men usually are. "I don't have that much confidence in what I believe," women frequently confess, and this self-doubt and lack of confidence causes women to avoid confrontation that requires them to reveal and stand by their basic beliefs. This is particularly true for women returning to work or to school after many years at home; awed by male authority figures, they tend to—as one described it—"go along with ideas that turn my stomach rather than risk a battle with someone who has more education and experience."

Values conflicts can help you overcome such handicaps. More than any other kind, they can offer you an opportunity to grow and help others grow in new directions. You can gain strength from them, and knowledge about yourself and others. Avoiding these conflicts will not make them go away, and may even aggravate differences and cause relationships to deteriorate.

It is a healthy sign that more and more women are gradually learning to trust their own perceptions of reality, and are gaining strength and courage to disclose and defend their own values.

How can you be sure you're heading for a values collision?

You feel unaccepting of the other's behavior.

The other person has resisted changing even after you've sent a Confrontive I-Message.

The other person does not see how changing her or his behavior tangibly or concretely affects you.

The other person does not consider that she or he has a problem, even though you do.

DEFINING THE VALUES DIFFERENCE

To deal with a values collision, the first step is to understand the real difference between you and the other person. I-Messages and Active Listening are the most effective ways of defining the differences.

Often values differences first become apparent when:

You attempt to send a Confrontive I-Message and find it difficult to come up with a tangible effect of the other's behavior on you.

Your Confrontive I-Message doesn't work (i.e., the other person doesn't change).

The other person resists Method III conflict resolution.

A great many values collisions come about merely because of a lack of communication, a failure to disclose yourself. Very frequently, when you can clearly define a values difference, one or both of you learn something valuable, something important that you didn't know about the other person.

This step alone is often sufficient to reduce or resolve the values collision. When people can understand how deeply others feel about a value that they cherish and live by, and how they came to feel that way, they can empathize and become more tolerant of the others' values and behavior.

You can probably recall occasions in your life when this happened. You may have become friendly with someone who was extremely careful about money, maybe to the point of being stingy. At first her preoccupation with money irritated you. As you grew to know her better, you learned that she had been poor as a child. Then you found you could accept her frugality. She had not changed, and maybe never would, but your view of her—your attitude —was altered. An adjustment took place within you that deepened your capacity for understanding and compassion.

We can see how this works in the case of a woman whose husband retired at a time when her career was reaching its peak:

"I hesitated to discuss my work with him, because I was afraid it would make him feel even more out of things. Underneath my hesitation was the feeling that he didn't really approve of my career, and I was sure he resented the fact that I was now providing the financial support for the two of us. As a result, our relationship became strained—you know how it is when you try to avoid talking about something that's important to you. It all came to a head when he confronted me, said how much it hurt him to be left out of a big chunk of my life. I Active Listened and found out he was really interested in my work and proud of my achievements—and was even able to accept the financial situation."

This step of defining values differences can be especially significant when you have continually tried to adapt yourself to others' values and have not stood up for your own. It may take lots of time and reflection to become aware of some of the ideas and beliefs you deeply value, and to get the courage to express them in clear, certain, disclosing ways, especially to people who have come to expect you to think and behave in particular ways.

WAYS OF COPING WITH CONFLICTS OF VALUES

In the E.T.W. course we teach several ways for women to learn to cope with values collisions in their relationships—ways that do not involve giving in or adapting to the other's values unwillingly. These are:

Learning to live with the differences

Modifying yourself

Using Method III to problem-solve the other's unacceptable *behavior*, not change the value

Trying to influence the other's values

Altering the relationship

Learning to Live with the Differences

Do you find it hard to accept someone who chooses to be different from you, or whose view of reality is different from yours? Someone whose perceptions are different from yours? If so, why? Must people be carbon copies of you for you to like them? The fact is, you *can* be accepting of others. You can recognize that there will always be value differences between you and other people.

There is much to be said for learning to live with values differences. Incompatible values are by no means necessarily a reason for breaking up a friendship, a marriage, or a professional relationship. Value differences can add excitement, interest, and stimulation to our personal dealings; they can keep relationships from becoming boring (as they so often are when people completely agree with each other). In some marriages and friendships people thrive on a lifetime debate that's never resolved, and never loses its challenge for both parties.

Modifying Yourself: Changing Your Own Values

When it's clear to you what the differences are, can you reconsider your values and perhaps move closer to the other person's? Are you willing to "try on" the other's value and possibly make some changes in the way you think?

Modifying yourself is really a form of self-development. You're saying, in effect: "I have my own ideas, but yours may be just as valid, maybe more so. I'm willing to listen —and be open to them."

It is essential that you do this *willingly;* it's important that your decision to change a value be based on your desire to do so, not to give in to (or accommodate) someone else. Self-modification is effective only when the change comes about as part of a learning process and is genuine. Trying to force yourself to adopt attitudes or make changes in yourself that are not natural to you will probably fail, and will have destructive effects on you and your relationships.

Clinging to outgrown values keeps us from experiencing new and exciting ways of thinking and acting. This does not mean that values built up over a lifetime should (or can) be drastically revised. It does suggest that an open, accepting look at new ideas is essential to healthy growth.

A woman who changed her religious affiliation reports:

"I converted to my husband's religion when we married. It was only a formality on my part, because I'd never been especially religious. But as I learned more about my adopted faith, I became interested in it. My husband died last year, but I continue to observe the rituals and ceremonies. It's comforting to me and gives me a feeling of belonging."

Converting to another religion or switching to another political party are fairly extreme ways of modifying oneself; slight, gradual changes are more common. To modify yourself, consider these possibilities:

You can change your position on issues. Regardless of how convinced you are that your view is the correct one, do some research on the arguments of the opposing side. Try to get as much information as you can on both sides, then reevaluate your position and take into account what you've learned.

You can question the usefulness of your values and reexamine critically their true and current importance to you. Are you clinging to them out of habit or stubbornness, or do they really serve an essential purpose for you now?

You can ask yourself whether you have exclusive access to the truth about such matters as cultural tastes, lifestyles, work habits, religion, politics, dress, morals.

You can examine whether you really like people in general, or only particular types of people. Do you automatically reject the values of people you don't like?

You can become more accepting of yourself. If you like yourself, it'll be easier for you to like others. Recent research findings have demonstrated a close relationship between acceptance of self and acceptance of others. If you're impatient with yourself, you're likely to be rigid and impatient with others.

You can learn more about others who are different from you. There's plenty of evidence that knowing someone better increases liking and acceptance, and decreases fear and rejection.

When you do want to modify your values, it's important that you keep in touch with yourself and the changes taking place within you. As one way of doing this, you might want to test yourself from time to time to see whether you "Strongly Agree," "Agree," "Disagree," or "Strongly Disagree" with such value-laden statements as:

A woman's place is in the home.

Women are more effective in dealing with young children than men are.

Men and women should have the same legal rights.

Quotas for equal employment of minorities and women should be required of all employers.

Birth-control devices should be available to anyone at any age.

Both husband and wife should have an equal voice in money matters, even if only one has income.

Women are responsible for their own oppression; they can't blame men.

Men should have the final say-so in major family decisions.

In a divorce case, women should get custody of the children.

A woman should have the right to have an abortion.

Any sexual activity between consenting adults should be allowed.

Would your reactions have been the same five or ten years ago? How can you account for any changes that have taken place in what you believe? Who were the influencers, the people who helped shape your present-day values? Who are the people in your life today whose values are incompatible with yours? Can you live with the differences? If not, can you reduce those values differences by becoming more tolerant of their behavior?

Using Method III to Problem-Solve the Other's Unacceptable Behavior

Besides modifying yourself—or if you're unwilling or unable to change—you may want to try to get the other person at least to change her or his behavior, if not the value itself. This can make the values difference less upsetting and bothersome to you.

However, when we set out to try to change others with whom we are having a values conflict, we should first consider the risks. So much of human behavior is unpredictable that when we attempt to change someone we can never be sure where our efforts will lead. Values are particularly sensitive, because people do consider them so valuable, and perhaps even think of them as immutable eternal truths. There is always the danger that a relationship may be adversely affected when you try to jar such beliefs. A free-lance artist who always had a casual, easygoing lifestyle says:

"My girlfriend kept trying to turn me into a neat, orderly, punctual sort of guy. That's not the way I am or the way I want to be. I eventually found another girl who was willing to take me as I am."

It's possible for others to modify how they *behave* toward you even though their values have not changed at all. If you decide it's worth the risk to try to change the behavior of the other person, remember that Method III cannot be applied to an idea, style, or outlook but only to the specific *behavior* the other person uses to act out her or his value. Frequently you may find that as the other's behavior changes, the value difference becomes much less important. It may even disappear. More significantly, you may find that you no longer feel a need to change the other's value.

Value conflicts that might be resolved by problem-solving a change in behavior are:

Your friend makes a point of bringing her political beliefs, which are opposed to yours, into every conversation. She values her beliefs and has no intention of changing them, but agrees not to talk about them so much when you're together.

Your child's room is not up to your standards of neatness, so the two of you agree that she'll keep her door closed so you can't see inside.

Your husband enjoys the ethnic dishes his mother used to cook. At your marriage, she presented you with her recipes. You don't like this type of food, and also resent the time and work required to cook these dishes. Your husband agrees to have lunch at a restaurant near his office where they serve this food, or to learn to cook it himself.

You would like very much to learn to fly a plane. Your daughter is very frightened that you'll be hurt or killed. You agree to postpone learning to fly until she feels okay about it, or until she leaves home.

Just as in conflict-of-needs situations, these solutions must be agreed on by both people. Neither person should feel she or he has lost.

Such behavior changes tend to bring about feelings of reciprocation. Your willingness to change your own values-related behavior when it bothers someone greatly increases the chances that the other person will be open to changing her or his her behavior when it bothers or annoys you—a distinct benefit that can promote warmth throughout the relationship.

Trying to Influence the Other's Values

Getting others merely to change their *behavior* may not always be entirely satisfactory to you. You may still feel that it is important to you to change their *values.* Many people have a "missionary urge," the impulse to improve the lives of others. Probably few of us have not, at one time or another, thought the world would be a better place if only others shared our tastes and opinions on religious, political, or ethical issues. And there are times when changing the other's value seems like the only way out of an impasse.

As in self-modification, there obviously can be no quick and easy ways to change ideas that are important to other people. Long hours of study and counseling are usually required for a religious conversion. In the realms of politics, morals, and personal taste, people rarely switch from a "conservative" to a "liberal" position, or vice versa, without undergoing a series of experiences that gradually bring about a change in their values.

We teach two ways to influence another's values: modeling and consulting. These are very common ways of influencing people; they're constantly used in everyday activities and encounters. In both you're not attempting to influence others by using power or exercising any control over them.

MODELING

Acting as models for others is something we all do in one way or another, consciously or unconsciously. Just as others have influenced your ideas and actions, it's very likely that you have also been an influencer for others. Our earliest role models are, of course, parents and teachers who constantly set examples for us by what they believe and how they act on those beliefs. As we become adults and move away from home and school, other people—friends, spouses, coworkers—become examples for us to emulate. We, in turn, serve as models for them.

Living your values can be the most reliable way of imparting them to others. But how many people actually live by what they believe? For the most part, they profess loyalty to ideas and principles they may genuinely value very highly, yet the gap between what a person *says* and what she or he *does* often shows up like this:

Stated Value	*Actual Behavior*
People should participate in the affairs of their community.	Rarely takes the trouble to vote.
One should help the needy.	Never donates to charitable causes.
Religious or racial prejudice is shameful.	Belongs to a club that restricts membership.
It's important to protect the environment.	Always uses a car instead of taking the bus.
The aged deserve special consideration.	Can't find time to visit elderly parent in nursing home.

One should be sympathetic and helpful toward others who are in trouble.	Avoids getting involved in others' problems.
Self-disclosing communication is essential to good relationships.	Tells people what they want to hear.
Teenagers should not smoke pot, take drugs.	Parent drinks alcohol excessively.

If you really want others to follow your example, it's essential that you practice what you preach. "Do as I say, not as I do" is not an effective way to influence others. If you want the people you work with to be honest, you'll defeat your purpose by cheating on your expense account. If you'd like others to be punctual, better not keep them waiting. If you want to be treated as a professional person, don't dress seductively.

Today, as new choices open up for women, there is an increasing appreciation that the spread and visibility of positive feminine role models is slowly changing the values of society to accept women as full equals. When women were confined to homemaking, teaching, and nursing, those were the paths that most girls followed, regardless of their talents or ambitions. Beyond career choice, too, we have an opportunity to demonstrate to the people in our lives, regardless of gender, the values that are important to us.

CONSULTING

You can also influence the values of others by sharing your ideas, knowledge, and experience—acting as a "consultant."

A consultant, according to Webster, is "one who gives professional advice or services regarding matters in the field of [her or his] special knowledge or training." When you seek the services of a consultant, you're looking for help from someone with special expertise that you hope will be helpful to you. You enter into this relationship voluntarily, and though you expect to follow the advice you receive, you feel you have the option of rejecting it if it does not meet your needs.

This is the key to successful consulting—recognizing that the other is free to take your advice or leave it; that you're *sharing,* not *imposing; suggesting,* not *insisting* or even merely *preaching.*

Suppose you're marketing manager of a large corporation. You want to become more effective in the job and improve the performance of the division, so you hire a consultant. After several weeks of interviews with the staff, the consultant asks for a conference with you and tells you, the client:

"You'd be far more effective if you had weekly staff meetings. Research shows that work groups are from forty to fifty percent more productive when they have weekly staff meetings with their supervisor."

You think about the suggestion, but come to the conclusion that it's not in line with the needs of your division. A month later, you and your consultant have another meeting:

Consultant: I understand you've not had weekly staff meetings as I suggested. I told you that's necessary to make your division more effective. Why haven't you followed my recommendations?

You: I came to the conclusion that I didn't need weekly staff meetings because I have so many individual conferences.

Consultant: Individual meetings don't replace staff meetings. Apparently you're resisting my ideas. I can assure you that what I'm telling you is for your own good.

You: I appreciate that, but I feel I must follow my own judgment. After all, I'm the one who's responsible for the division.

Consultant: You have a strange way of carrying out your responsibilities. I warn you—you're heading for trouble. Do you realize you're behaving like a third-rate executive? You're not tuned in to the way things are done today. I predict you won't last very long in this job.

What do you think your reactions would be to this interview? How long would it take you to fire the consultant? In our personal relationships we also risk being "fired" when we're *aggressive* rather than *assertive* in offering advice to our friends, spouses, and children. Being effective as a consultant depends, first of all, on how you're perceived by other people. If they see you as someone with wisdom, expertise, experience, knowledge, sensitivity, sound values, clearly your potential as an influencer can be great. Aggressiveness diminishes effectiveness, as we've seen. And only an effective consultant leaves the door open for future opportunities, under other circumstances, to influence the thinking and behavior of others. To be an effective consultant:

Present supporting facts and figures and well-thought-out ideas.

Leave the responsibility for change ("buying" the consultant's ideas or beliefs) with the other person.

Don't hassle the other person. Try only once to influence—no more —unless there is a significant change in the circumstances (for example, you uncover new information) or she or he asks for more advice.

The essential skills of effective consulting are:

Clear presentation of your own values and why they're important to you (DECLARATIVE I-MESSAGES)

Active Listening to show acceptance of others' resistance to your values and their defense of their own values (SHIFTING GEAR)

This is how you might act as a consultant in a matter of personal values:

Objective	*Method*
Influence your friend to lose weight	Share your own experience with her, as well as books and articles about obesity
Encourage husband to change job	Find out about jobs you feel he would like and tell him about them
Discourage daughter from seeing boyfriend who is causing her unhappiness	Tell her about similar experience you had with a boy

Altering the Relationship

If none of your efforts resolves a values difference so you and the other person can live with it, you may be forced to change—or end the relationship. Although this is a very difficult decision to make, it can have very positive effects. Ending a destructive, dissatisfying relationship can be a big step in achieving your own identity and freedom to live in accordance with your own values and needs.

You may decide that, since you and your friend seem to spend most of your time arguing, you won't see each other so often in the future. If you find yourself locked into an unresolvable conflict with your supervisor, you might ask to be transferred to another department, or start looking for another job. If you and your husband have major problems and you see no hope of working them out, you may eventually decide you want a divorce. Do note, however, that people often choose to end relationships without fully exploring ways of working through their problems.

THE PROBLEM OF USING POWER TO RESOLVE VALUES COLLISIONS

Using power to influence the outcome of a values collision can be tempting, particularly as a shortcut if other available approaches are complex and time-consuming, and you hold most of the power in the relationship.

You can force your daughter to stay in college. You can insist that your subordinate dress differently. But, as most of us know, power tactics are often a costly way to preserve relationships. They're also unlikely to have any positive effect on the other person's values. In fact, the use of power in the area of values will practically guarantee being "fired" as a consultant.

When you act as an influencer through modeling and consulting, you're offering people an opportunity to change by encouraging an evolutionary process. The adaptations in their lives may be slow and gradual, but they will be lasting because they're not imposed; they're part of that person's learning and growth.

By exercising your influence, you're saying, in effect:

"I have no power over you, but here are the facts and figures that support my position. I leave responsibility for change with you. I won't hassle or nag if you don't make the changes I've suggested. I want to be influential and, above all, to preserve a good relationship with you. I accept the fact that the outcome of my consulting efforts is uncertain."

When you use power methods in a values collision you are denying people a chance to evolve at their own pace, in their own way. You're applying a "revolutionary" approach—instant change through coercion. The message you send comes through like this:

"I don't trust you to make this change on your own. I'll use whatever power is available to me to force the change—after all, it's for your own good."

Using power to alter another's values is frequently justified as being in the other's best interest. But consider what people throughout history have been forced to accept in the name of their "best interest"! That should give us pause when we set out to coerce change in others. Nonpower methods that people can adapt to their own needs and experience are more likely to yield change that's desired by you and truly accepted by the other person.

XII. MODIFYING THE ENVIRONMENT

Every change of scene becomes a delight.

SENECA

CHANGING or reshaping your physical surroundings can be a very effective way of preventing conflicts in your relationships and can sometimes resolve conflicts when Confrontive I-Messages and Active Listening don't work.

Suppose you want to relax by reading and your family is playing the stereo or watching television. You might choose to confront or model or consult, hoping to bring your family around to the joys of reading, but it would probably be more efficient to set up a reading corner for yourself in another room or suggest they move the stereo into another room.

The point is: all too often when we deal with other people we overlook the effect of the environments where we spend our lives. We often think about conflicts in such abstract ways that we overlook such simple solutions as doors that provide privacy; carpeting that muffles distracting noise; fences that reduce parental worry by keeping children safe from traffic.

Setting out to modify the environment is an assertive act: we make the determination to exercise control over our surroundings rather than letting our surroundings control us, and we take the initiative and responsibility for making the change. We should, of course, be prepared to problem-solve if physical modifications involve needs or interests of others. Method III usually helps.

Among the many other ways for you, your family,

and/or your coworker to brainstorm your particular needs, here are eight major ways to modify the environment and resolve or reduce conflicts:

Enriching

Enlarging

Impoverishing

Restricting

Simplifying

Rearranging

Systematizing

Anticipating

Here are some examples of each.

ENRICHING

This means adding materials or activities to the environment to make it more interesting and stimulating.

Some ways of enriching your home environment might be:

Inviting people you'd like to get to know to dinner

Signing up for interesting classes

Learning new games or other activities together

Having debates about subjects of mutual interest

Providing games, puzzles, books, records

Going to an interesting place on the weekend (zoo, park, camping, skating, bicycling, etc.)

Doing a project together—starting a small vegetable garden, building a doghouse, researching your family history

Examples of enriching your work environment might include:

Setting up a table and chairs where employees could have lunch and relax during breaks

Installing a coffee or tea machine

Providing/requesting modern office equipment for employees

Providing educational opportunities, such as inviting outside consultants to come and speak

Starting training programs for education and advancement

Obtaining more up-to-date books and materials in your field

Providing/requesting space and/or equipment for physical exercise for employees

Providing/requesting facilities for the care of small children

Bringing in plants, pictures to enhance the office

ENLARGING

Experiments have shown that crowding and density are often responsible for antisocial behavior. You can sometimes relieve stress and tension by expanding access to the environment, increasing the availability of space. At home the remedies could include:

Taking out a partition or wall to make a room more spacious

Adding a room to be used for work, play, storage, etc.

Replacing a double bed with a convertible sofa

Selecting furniture that has more than one use—for example, a table for dining, sewing, playing games

Selecting furniture that can be folded and put away—for example, folding tables and chairs

Renting outside storage space

At work some ideas are:

Providing more work space for certain employees

Removing doors

Taking out useless partitions

Renting outside storage space

Buying office furniture that offers several uses—desks for typing, writing, collating, etc.

IMPOVERISHING

This includes removing materials, objects, and activities from the environment; decreasing stimulation. When the environment is overly rich, people can be overloaded with demands and made irritable and anxious.

Some at-home examples are:

Not taking phone calls during dinner or conversations

Cutting down on outside activities—trips, parties, classes, shopping

Turning down (or off) radios, stereos, televisions

Relaxing quietly—thinking, reading, napping, chatting

Using only certain rooms for watching TV, listening to radio, etc.

Using headphones to listen to music

At work, examples include:

Not taking phone calls during meetings

Scheduling fewer meetings

Placing Xerox machine in another area

Using earplugs in noisy office

Arranging to work at home or elsewhere when you require uninterrupted concentration

RESTRICTING

This involves limiting or controlling access to the environment; controlling the availability of resources, physical area, or activities.

In your home this might include:

Installing doors to rooms where you want privacy

Agreeing on rooms to which it's acceptable to bring food

Putting valuable objects out of reach

Putting dangerous household supplies (soap, disinfectants, poisons) out of reach of children and pets

Building a fence around the yard

Installing wooden gates at top and bottom of stairs to prevent small children from climbing them

Installing locks on gates

At work some examples of restricting the environment could include:

Assigning employee parking places

Installing partitions between working areas to cut down on noise

SIMPLIFYING

Reducing the complexity of equipment and activities can sometimes be helpful to avoid disputes at work and at home.
Some suggestions for simplifying your home life are:

Putting work supplies where everyone can readily find and reach them

Keeping pens and pads near telephone

Putting an alarm clock in each bedroom

Instructing family members where supplies are kept—sheets, towels, tissues, etc.

Instructing family members in the proper use of household appliances —washer, dryer, stove, iron, blender, etc.

Having a system for taking phone messages

Arranging car pools

Giving away or selling unused clothes, furniture, etc.

Ways to simplify the operation of your office include:

Keeping office supplies in easily accessible place

Replacing obsolete systems with new, more workable ones: filing, mailing lists, etc.

Instructing office staff in proper use of office equipment—copying machine, coffeepot, etc.

Storing or throwing out old files, papers, etc.

REARRANGING

By altering the position of objects or the schedule of activities, it's possible to improve the way people relate to each other.

At home rearranging could include:

Rearranging furniture to get more privacy—or to provide a conversation or play area

Reorganizing the kitchen and/or other rooms to make them more functional

Changing the time you have dinner so your family can watch a favorite TV program

Rescheduling your weekend trip so some friends can join you

At work they might be:

Placing people who work together in the same room or area

Arranging chairs in a circle for meetings

Rescheduling a meeting so more people can attend

SYSTEMATIZING

You can organize, schedule, and coordinate objects or activities more systematically so they'll function more efficiently.

Some at-home suggestions are:

Setting up a message center, perhaps a bulletin board

Providing a big calendar for family's use in making plans

Installing hooks throughout the house for clothing, towels, utensils, etc.

Keeping a handy list of phone numbers and addresses of frequently called friends and relatives

Providing a pad for adding items to the grocery list (and other shopping lists)

Creating a better way to keep records of expenses and income; setting up a budget

Organizing your books by subject or author

At work some examples are:

Creating new systems for filing, mailing, ordering, shipping, etc.

Scheduling lunch hours at different times

Sharing more information with others so work isn't duplicated

Keeping your personal calendar up-to-date for scheduling appointments, etc.

ANTICIPATING

Some conflicts can be prevented by advance planning.

Some suggestions for planning ahead in your home are:

Lining up alternative vacation plans in case the trip your family has been counting on doesn't work out

Having your husband check his calendar before ordering tickets in advance

Giving your family a copy of your job travel schedule as far in advance as possible

Childproofing your home before your friends with young children arrive for a visit

Marking on your calendar the birthdays and anniversaries of friends and family so you can buy cards or gifts for these occasions at your leisure

Informing your children of the date you've set for a party, or when you're going out for an evening

Stocking up on food, etc., for special occasions—holidays, birthday parties

Keeping change in a kitchen drawer for lunches, laundry, emergencies, etc.

Keeping an extra key to the house hidden outside

Keeping a phone number available for your children to call in case of emergency

Keeping frozen foods for quick, easy preparation

Informing your group ahead of time when you won't attend the next meeting

Planning ahead in the office:

Having coworkers check calendars before scheduling important meetings

Informing coworkers when you expect clients to visit the office

Informing coworkers when you plan to be out of the office—on business, vacation, etc.

Providing the phone number of someone your office staff can call in case you have an emergency—your doctor, spouse, child, friend, etc.

Informing coworkers in advance when you won't attend a scheduled meeting

Environmental modification not only takes some problems out of your relationships; it also heightens your awareness of yourself in relation to your world. Surroundings tend to become overly familiar to us, so we become, in a sense, blinded to our work and play settings. By making a conscious decision to change these settings, we begin to look at the physical world in a different way, becoming newly aware of the many ways it can be changed or adapted to meet human needs—our own and those of others.

XIII. HELPING ANOTHER PERSON WITH A PROBLEM

You can't give people pride, but you can provide the kind of understanding that makes people look to their inner strengths and find their own sense of pride.

CHARLESZETTA WADDLES

WHAT about times when someone with whom you have a relationship has a problem, is troubled, or has unmet needs? Now the area in the Behavior Rectangle you want to concentrate on is the top part—when the other person owns a problem:

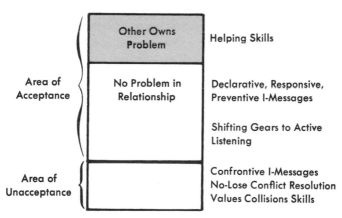

When another person has a problem independently of you, it falls within your area of acceptance, making it possible for you to offer your help freely and willingly. Often—but not always in your close relationships: with your spouse, children, friends, relatives, coworkers—you may want to try to help others work through their difficulties. In E.T.W. we teach some specific skills for doing this. But first let's examine what many of us do when we mean to be helpful.

INEFFECTIVE RESPONSES WHEN ANOTHER PERSON OWNS A PROBLEM: THE ROADBLOCKS TO COMMUNICATION

When another person owns (is experiencing) a problem and you've decided to offer your help, it may be tempting to try to help solve the problem by giving good advice, asking questions, or offering reassurance. Often, we use these responses because we feel we should have the answers and should solve the problem ourselves. Or we get so uncomfortable seeing others, especially our children, feel troubled and upset that we want to help them get rid of their problems quickly.

Such helping attempts, well intentioned as they may be, generally do more harm than good and impede the flow of communication from the person with the problem.

Here are the responses that act as Roadblocks to Communication to people with problems:

1. Ordering, Directing, Commanding

"Stop crying!"

"Don't worry so much."

"Quit your griping!"

"Go get your work done."

"Get your mind off it."

These responses tell others what to do by giving them orders or commands. In effect, you tell others that their feelings or needs are not important; they must comply with what you feel or need. You communicate unacceptance of others as they are at the moment. These messages engender feelings of resentment or anger, frequently causing others to express hostility, fight back, resist, or test your will. These messages may also suggest that you don't trust the others' judgment or competence.

2. Warning, Admonishing, Threatening

"You'd better apologize to him or you'll be sorry later."

"If you don't stop drinking, you're going to lose your job."

"If you don't start working harder in that class, you're going to fail."

"If you come to work late after this, you're going to be in serious trouble."

These messages tell others what consequences will occur if they do or don't do something, and can make them fearful and submissive. These messages cause resentment and hostility in the same way that ordering, directing, and commanding do. People sometimes respond to warnings or threats by feeling or saying, "I don't care what happens, I still feel this way." These messages also invite others to test your firmness, perhaps by doing something they've been warned against—just to see if the promised consequences actually happen.

3. Moralizing, Preaching, Obliging

"You should never lie."

"I think you're obligated to go."

"You ought to help her out."

"You should have told me this a long time ago."

"Do unto others as you would have them do unto you."

Telling others what they should or ought to do is seldom helpful. Such messages bring to bear on others the pressure of external authority, duty, or obligation. People frequently respond to such "shoulds," "oughts," and "musts" by resisting and defending their own postures even more strongly. These messages communicate to others that you do not trust their ability to judge ideas and values for themselves, that they had better accept what "others" deem right. They may also cause feelings of guilt in others, making them feel they're "bad."

4. Advising, Giving Suggestions or Solutions

"I think it'd be good for you to think this over for a few days."

"Why don't you just try to find another job!"

"The best thing for you to do is just forget it ever happened."

"I think you should consider getting a divorce."

"Why don't you just decide to stop smoking if you're so worried about it?"

A common response to another's problem is telling her or him exactly how to solve it. Others often regard this as evidence that you don't have confidence in their judgment or their ability to find their own solutions. Such messages may also encourage others to become dependent on you and stop thinking for themselves. People often strongly resent the attitude of superiority that advising or suggesting implies. Or they feel inferior and think,

"Why didn't I think of that?" They may sigh and say, "You always know better than I what to do." Also, advice may make the other person feel that you don't understand the real problem.

5. Persuading with Logic, Arguing, Instructing, Lecturing

"Let me show you where you're wrong."

"I know I'm right about this."

"Let me teach you something about getting along with men."

"My experience tells me that won't work!"

"Don't you know that . . ."

These are attempts to influence others with facts, counterarguments, logic, information, or your own opinions. When you take on a helping role, it's difficult to stop instructing or using logical arguments, yet this kind of "teaching" often makes others feel you're trying to make them look inferior, subordinate, or inadequate. Logic and facts often make others defensive and resentful. People seldom like to be shown they're wrong. It makes them defend their positions even more strongly. People also tend to view lectures as hassling, and tune out quickly. They often go to great lengths to discount your "facts." They may even ignore facts and assume an "I don't care" attitude.

6. Judging, Criticizing, Disagreeing, Blaming

"Now look what you've done!"

"If you weren't so self-indulgent, you could stop drinking."

"You're one of the laziest people I have ever seen!"

"If you'd done it right the first time, this wouldn't have happened!"

Hearing others' problems often propels us into making negative judgments or evaluations of them. These messages, probably more than any of the others, make people feel inadequate, inferior, stupid, unworthy, or bad. Our judgments and evaluations help shape others' self concepts. As we judge others, so will they often judge themselves. Negative criticism also evokes countercriticism: "You're not so hot yourself" or "Since when were you perfect?" Evaluation strongly influences people to keep their feelings to themselves. They quickly learn that it isn't safe to reveal their problems and share their troubles; people hate to be judged negatively, and they respond defensively to protect their self-images. Often they become angry and feel hostile toward you even if your evaluation happens to be correct.

7. Praising, Agreeing, Evaluating Positively, Approving

"Well, *I* think you did a really good job."

"You're one of the few women who could have done that."

"You have so much potential."

"I think you used very good judgment."

"You work so well under pressure."

We often think that a positive evaluation or judgment will help people get over a problem. Contrary to the common belief that praise is always beneficial, it often has

very negative effects when others are experiencing problems. A positive evaluation that does not fit the other
person's self-image may evoke hostility ("I am *not* a good
dancer" or "My hair looks *awful* this way, I *hate* my
hair").

People also infer that if we can judge them positively,
we can just as easily judge them negatively some other
time. Also, if praise is frequent, its absence may be interpreted as criticism when it's not given. Praise given to one
person may be interpreted by others as a negative evaluation of them—that, comparatively speaking, they're not
so good. Praise, therefore, tends to promote competition
for recognition or the need to score Brownie points.

Praise is often felt to be manipulative, a subtle way of
influencing others to do what you want them to do:
"You're just saying that so I'll work harder." Praise frequently embarrasses people, especially when given in
front of others. If you praise, you run the risk of making
people become so dependent on it that they cannot function without constant approval from you.

8. Name-calling, Ridiculing, Shaming

"You're such a stickler for accuracy!"

"You're so nosy!"

"You're a male-chauvinist pig!"

"You're a sore loser!"

"You're so compulsive about neatness!"

These responses make others feel they're foolish, bad,
or wrong. Such messages can have very damaging effects
on another's self-image. People most frequently respond

to such messages by giving one back to you: "Boy, what a grouch!" or "Look who's calling who lazy!" Name-calling can provoke so much defensiveness that others will focus on arguing and fighting back, rather than taking a close look at themselves. "I am not inconsiderate . . . you expect too much!"

9. Interpreting, Analyzing, Diagnosing

"You're doing that to get attention."

"You're just jealous."

"You're trying to get back at me for what I said yesterday."

"I can see you have problems with authority figures."

"You wouldn't have said that to a woman!"

These responses tell others what their motives are or analyze why they're doing or saying something, .communicating that you have them figured out or diagnosed. Such messages can be very threatening to other people. If the analysis is accurate, the person may feel embarrassed at being "exposed"; if the analysis is wrong, as it often is, the other person will become angry at being unjustly accused. We often communicate that we feel superior to other people when we analyze and diagnose, an attitude that the other person resents. These messages tend to cut off further communication from others; they learn to stop sharing feelings with you.

10. Reassuring, Sympathizing, Consoling, Supporting

"You'll feel better about it tomorrow."

"You'll find somebody else—he wasn't your type anyway."

"You'll get over it—just give yourself time."

"Don't worry, I know you'll do a good job."

"Things will work out for the best—you'll see."

It's tempting to try to make others feel better by talking them out of their feelings, minimizing their difficulties away, denying the seriousness of their problems. These messages are not as helpful as most of us think. To reassure a person when she or he is feeling disturbed may only convince her or him that you don't understand. ("You wouldn't say that if you knew how scared I am.")

We often reassure others because we're not comfortable with hearing their strong feelings; we want to avoid hearing more. Such messages tell others that you want them to stop feeling a certain way. People can easily see through reassurances as a subtle and indirect attempt to change them.

11. Probing, Questioning, Interrogating

"When did you first start thinking about this?"

"Who talked you into doing such a thing?"

"Why are you just now bringing this up?"

"What are you going to do about it?"

"Does your boss know about this?"

These responses are efforts to find reasons, motives, causes, or to get more information to help you solve the other's problem. Yet often questions convey your lack of trust, your suspicion or doubt. People also interpret some questions as attempts to "get them out on a limb." ("How much beer do you drink a day? A six-pack? Well, no wonder you're gaining weight!")

People often feel threatened by questions, especially when they don't understand why they're being questioned. Think of how often people answer your question with a question of their own: "Why are you asking?" or "What are you driving at?" A defensive response to questions is the ubiquitous "I don't know." If you question people who share a problem with you, they usually infer that you're gathering data to solve their problems for them, rather than letting them find their own solutions. People generally do not want us to come up with answers to their problems.

When you ask a question of someone who is talking about a problem, each question limits the person's freedom to talk about whatever she or he wants to; in a sense, each question dictates her or his next message. If you ask, "When did you first notice this feeling?" you're asking the person to talk only about the onset of the feeling, nothing else.

12. Withdrawing, Distracting, Humoring

"Let's go have a nice dinner and forget about it."

"Let's discuss this later."

"You think you've got problems!"

"What you're saying reminds me of problems I've had in the past."

"Let's talk about something more pleasant."

This category includes messages that convey a desire to withdraw from the problem yourself, a wish to distract the other away from her or his problems through kidding or pushing the problem aside. Such messages can communicate that you're not interested in others, don't respect their feelings, perhaps even reject them. People are generally quite serious and intent when they need to talk about something. When you respond with kidding you can make them feel hurt, rejected, belittled. Putting people off or diverting their feelings may for the moment appear successful, but a person's feelings do not always go away. They often come up again later.

We're not suggesting that these twelve responses be permanently dropped from your communication with others. While they're best avoided when another person owns a problem, many of them are not damaging and are even helpful and effective when your relationships are in the No-Problem Area.

FIVE IMPORTANT ELEMENTS FOR BEING AN EFFECTIVE HELPER

When you act as a helping agent for another person, you create an opportunity to boost a person's growth and healthful change. And when you succeed in helping someone important in your life, your investment of time, skill, and thoughtfulness usually rewards you with a deeper and more enduring relationship.

What do you need to provide the kind of assistance that will have a positive effect on those who come to you for help with their problems? Social scientists who researched this question found you need at least five primary characteristics to be an effective helping agent:

Acceptance

Empathy

Genuineness

A degree of personal fulfillment

A feeling of reciprocity

Acceptance

This means allowing others to be what they are; not demanding that they start thinking or behaving differently or in ways that are out of harmony with who they really are. Accepting others does not mean you must abandon your critical judgments or place others' values before your own. It does mean that, to be of assistance to them, you're willing to view them and their concerns in a positive or neutral way, and let the responsibility for solving their problems rest with them. Your attitude could be expressed as follows:

"I want to respond to your request for help. Therefore, I am making a conscious decision to put my value judgments aside so I can identify with you as closely as possible—accepting you as you are now."

Empathy

In identifying with another, you achieve a vicarious experience of the other's feelings; you put yourself in the other person's shoes. When we empathize with others, we use our own experience to identify with their feelings or with their reactions to the particular circumstances in their lives. An empathic response to another is based on similarities between us. Empathy is creative, because it requires an act of imagination that projects us into the inner world of others. Even though we may not have experienced exactly what they're going through, if we can identify with them very closely, we can understand with empathy. For example, even though you've never been fired, you can understand how your husband feels when he gets fired.

Genuineness

This means having an honest, open relationship with the other person. It also includes being trustworthy. Before we can help others, they must first of all believe in us. When you come across in any way as phony, there's little you can do or say to assist others; they'll be suspicious of your sincerity.

To be self-disclosing is important in a helping relationship; through revealing ourselves we learn the extent to which we're similar to—or different from—the other person, and then can relate more fully to the other's needs through a better understanding of our own.

Others must be able to count on your not divulging confidential information, not making fun of them, not using what they tell you against them later. They must be able to trust that you'll be willing to confront them when you have problems with the way they act.

A Degree of Personal Fulfillment

While acceptance, empathy, and genuineness are clearly desirable, without a feeling of personal fulfillment you will probably not feel much like being in the helping role—at least not on a continuing basis.

Let's consider the experience of Helen, who had established her own public-relations agency by the time she was 30. After her marriage and the birth of her first child, she sold the business and determined to devote herself to her family. "I adored my husband and child, but I desperately missed the excitement and the sense of personal achievement I'd had from my work."

As the years passed, and two more children were born, she tried to compensate for her feelings of guilt and frustration by increasingly strenuous, sometimes fanatic, efforts on behalf of her family. "I took on all their problems and couldn't understand why, most of the time, my getting involved only made things worse. I began to think of myself as a failure. What good was I if I wasn't any real use to the people I cared about most in the world?"

By attempting to fulfill herself through her family, Helen neglected to examine some of her own important personal needs. While we want to serve others, to be nurturing and supportive to them, so often we find ourselves with a sense of frustration, which psychotherapist Jean Baker Miller describes as arising from "doing good and feeling bad." When we've tried so hard and given so much of ourselves, why, we wonder, are the results so poor?

Helping others is not a substitute for meeting one's own needs. If we think of it that way, we will often feel resentful and angry at our incompleteness. We can't be very effective helping agents for others if some of our own important needs are not met. There must be a balance between the two. To be truly effective helping agents, we must have some degree of satisfaction and fulfillment in our own lives.

A Feeling of Reciprocity

Last, we must feel that when we help someone with problems, the relationship is reciprocal—at least to some extent.

You've probably had the experience of freely and willingly listening and helping a friend solve some of her or his problems and then finding that when you had one, she or he wasn't willing to listen to you. You may have felt cheated, and found yourself feeling less willing to listen to her or him later.

We need to feel that our relationships are fair, reciprocal, cooperative (even when it comes to helping). The
attitude could be expressed like this:

"I'm willing to try to help when you have problems, and I'd like
to feel you'd do the same for me."

PASSIVE LISTENING RESPONSES

When others give you a clue (verbal and/or nonverbal) that they're experiencing problems, one effective
way to help them handle upset feelings is with Passive
Listening responses. They show your acceptance and acknowledgment and encourage the upset person to continue communicating. Passive Listening responses are:

Attending

Silence

Acknowledgments

Door Openers

Attending

This means being physically with the other person
when she or he expresses a problem. You demonstrate
your willingness to listen by staying in the same room, not
busying yourself with other tasks, facing the other person,
and maintaining constant eye contact.

Silence

Your ability to remain silent or passively listen when the
other person expresses a problem can be very helpful and
encouraging, especially when the other person is just beginning to share a problem, or when she or he is ex-

periencing a strong or deep feeling, such as sadness, fear, or hopelessness.

Acknowledgments

These are brief expressions that indicate you're paying attention. To some extent, they also communicate your acceptance and empathy. They include such responses as:

"Hm-hmm."

"I see."

"I hear you."

"Oh."

"Uh-huh."

"Really."

"I sure understand that."

Door Openers

These responses invite the other person to say more, to expand her or his thoughts, ideas, and feelings. They demonstrate your acceptance and communicate your willingness to try to help.

"Do you want to tell me about it?"

"I'd like to know more about how you feel."

"Would you like to talk about it?"

"Can I help?"

"Let's discuss it."

"I'd like to hear more about how you feel."

"You seem really quiet tonight—is something bothering you?"

While these Passive Listening skills are effective in making the other person feel accepted and in keeping communication flowing, their usefulness for communicating, understanding, and facilitating a resolution of the other's problem is sometimes limited. You'll need to employ a way of responding that requires a much more active role in the communication process—Active Listening.

ACTIVE LISTENING

You're already familiar with Active Listening in the context of shifting gears to help reduce resistance to your I-Messages. It's also an essential skill for helping others when they own a problem. In fact, you'll find it's your principal way to communicate acceptance and empathy when you're in the helping role. Although the skill remains the same, you assume a totally different posture when you use it to help someone else, not like your posture for shifting gears to help you meet your own needs. Recall how the communications diagram works (for complete description, refer back to Chapter III):

YOUR FRIEND'S MESSAGE (SENDER)
"You know I've been feeling this way now for two weeks. It should be gone by now. What would cause this sort of fatigue?"

worried — encoding

she's worried — decoding

SENDER

"You sound worried that something may be seriously wrong with you."
YOUR ACTIVE LISTENING FEEDBACK

While learning to be a good listener is not easy, we know that, given time and patience, this important skill can be learned and used effectively. When we ask women to tell us specific changes in the way they act—changes resulting from the E.T.W. course—we hear over and over again such comments as:

"Active Listening has improved my relationship with my husband. He's much more open with me."

"I've learned new things about people I thought I knew like a book."

"Active Listening made me much more aware of the needs and feelings of others."

"Since I started Active Listening to her, my daughter and I have grown much closer."

"Active Listening with my seven-year-old is bringing about better conversation."

"I helped make a person feel much better by our session. I feel closer to her as a result. I also feel like a burden has been lifted from me."

Here is an actual session that shows how Active Listening worked in a helping relationship between two friends:

Joan: (Big sigh, frown)

Valerie: You look upset. Would you like to tell me about it?

Joan: I feel so discouraged! I don't know how to put it into words.

Valerie: Mm-hum.

Joan: I thought this last job was really the one for me.

Valerie: It was the kind of job you'd been hoping for.

Joan: My skills and qualifications are exactly what they needed. I figured I could really go places in that organization.

Valerie: (Sympathetic nod)

Joan: When I found out the director was being transferred to the Ohio office, I thought I had a pretty good chance for the job. Of course, they never before promoted a woman to that level.

Valerie: You thought being a woman might keep you from getting the job.

Joan: Yeah—but I thought I could make the breakthrough. But I didn't think I could do it without the support of Bill Lester, who was in charge of that division.

Valerie: To have any chance at all, you'd need his help . . .

Joan: Yeah, so I began being extra friendly to him, if you know what I mean. And it seemed to be working. He asked me to lunch a couple of times. Then we started meeting for drinks after work. And once, when his wife was out of town, we had dinner and went to a movie. It was all nice and friendly. Mostly, we talked about work—but he kept telling me how much he admired my work. I thought I had the promotion sewed up.

Valerie: You were pretty sure of it.

Joan: He gave me some fairly strong hints . . . and then, well, they started gossiping at the office, and I guess his wife heard about it. Anyway, next thing I knew,

I was told by Personnel that they were making some changes and they would no longer need me. Just like that, out of the blue.

Valerie: It came as a real shock to you.

Joan: It knocked me over! I tried talking to Bill Lester about it—but he was suddenly unavailable. And you know something, I had a similar experience in the two jobs I had before that one.

Valerie: In those jobs, you also thought you had to get friendly with the higher-ups in order to advance.

Joan: Well, it's not easy for a woman to make it into management. You have to pull a few strings.

Valerie: You don't feel as though you can count on your ability and training alone.

Joan: Well, I just assumed I could move up the ladder a lot faster if I got on the right side of the right people. But you know, I guess I was underrating myself. Didn't really have confidence in my ability to make it on my own. I'm beginning to see it—I've been sort of following a pattern.

Valerie: You're feeling maybe you don't need to "play the game" anymore. You feel stronger about yourself now.

Joan: Yeah . . . I can tell you—next job I get, it's going to be different. I don't know why it didn't occur to me before. Thanks for listening.

GUIDELINES FOR USING ACTIVE LISTENING EFFECTIVELY

Active Listening is the skill that many women say is the most difficult to use. While some people are just naturally empathic listeners, most of us need considerable practice before we feel comfortable actively listening. In the meantime, it may seem contrived to both you and others.

Also, people sometimes respond negatively when someone attempts to Active Listen—they get angry, feel used, or feel something is being done to them. They feel put in an inferior position, that they're being "treated" or "doctored." Here are some of their negative responses:

"Don't use that stuff on me!"

"Why are you talking that way?"

"I don't want you to listen, I just want an answer to my question."

"That sounds so phony!"

"Oh, so you've found another technique to use on us!"

"That's what I just told you! I don't need you to say the same thing right back to me!"

These protests often mean that Active Listening has been misused. It's not a "technique" to be applied every time another person says something. Here are guidelines for the best use of Active Listening:

Use Active Listening principally when you hear a *problem* and get the impression the person wants to talk about it. It's inappropriate to use Active Listening when people have problem-free conversations about the weather, current events, work, vacation plans, etc.

Use Active Listening to help another only when you're in the mood and have time to listen. If you're feeling upset or impatient (or are preoccupied with your own problems), you won't come across as accepting and empathic.

Make good use of the Passive Listening skills (Attending, Silence, Acknowledgment, and Door Openers). Not every statement from the other person needs an Active Listening feedback. Use Active Listening primarily when feelings are *intense* and the other person's need to be heard is *unmistakable*.

Sometimes you can give the other person information she or he wants. But first be sure you listened long enough to be certain you understand what the real problem is and that the other person wants the information you're offering.

Be prepared for the rejection of any suggestions or advice you might offer—they may be neither appropriate nor helpful.

Don't *impose* Active Listening on the other person. Be sensitive to cues that tell you the person you're trying to help doesn't want to pursue a problem or has finished talking about it.

Don't use Active Listening in a manipulative way—perhaps to get specific information to use later against the other.

Don't use Active Listening to avoid self-disclosure.

Don't use Active Listening to avoid conflict.

Don't fall into the habit of always using such common phrases as "Sounds like you . . ." and "I hear you saying . . ." to start your Active Listening responses. If you do, others will begin to regard those words as mechanical, even manipulative.

Don't use it to demonstrate what a skilled listener you are.

Don't expect the other person to arrive at some preferred solution you have in mind. Active Listening is a tool for helping people find their own unique solutions.

Don't expect (or insist) that the other person arrive at a solution at all. A solution may not emerge until later, and sometimes a person may never tell you how the problem was eventually resolved.

COMMON ACTIVE LISTENING ERRORS

When people experience repeated failures with Active Listening, we usually find they have either failed to stay in touch with the sender's feelings or have not been able to keep their own feelings out of the listening process.

To illustrate how Active Listening can be off target, here are some of the most common errors, with examples. Let's say your coworker sends you the following message:

"I wish Sally weren't such a gossip. It's causing trouble for her at the office."

Your Feedback to Coworker	Error
"You despise Sally."	*Overshooting.* Exaggerating the emotional level.
"You're not fond of Sally's conversation."	*Undershooting:* Diluting the emotional intensity.
"You wish she'd get out of your life."	*Adding:* Generalizing or expanding the scope of the other's message.
"Sally bothers you."	*Omitting:* Reducing or skipping pertinent facts.
"You're cooking up a scheme to get back at her."	*Rushing:* Anticipating the sender's next thoughts.
"You were saying earlier that Sally and you have always been cool to each other."	*Lagging:* Being out of phase with the sender's message. Backtracking or failure to keep up.
"You're sort of paranoid about people talking behind your back."	*Analyzing:* Interpreting underlying motives.
"You wish Sally weren't such a gossip—it's causing trouble for her at the office."	*Parroting:* Word-for-word repetition.

It won't be difficult to know when you make these errors; the other will let you know when your feedback is not accurate.

While Active Listening is a technique, a skill to be learned, remember that its main purpose is as a vehicle for communicating your acceptance, empathy, and understanding of others. The more your attitude can be one of acceptance, the less Active Listening will seem like a technique.

XIV. PLANNING FOR PERSONAL EFFECTIVENESS

*Discoveries have reverberations. A new idea about oneself
or some aspect of one's relations to others unsettles all
one's other ideas, even the superficially related ones. No
matter how slightly, it shifts one's entire orientation. And
somewhere along the line of consequences, it changes one's
behavior.*

PATRICIA McLAUGHLIN

A final, essential step in taking more responsibility
for your own life and getting more of your needs met is
planning—an activity of free, self-directed individuals
that implies you're capable of thinking and behaving in an
unrestricted way; that you, not external forces, are deciding how you will act. When you make plans and proceed
to carry them out, you're saying, in effect: "Out of all the
choices, alternatives, directions, and opportunities available for me, I'll consciously choose those that most accurately reflect my needs, values, and goals. In making these
choices, I will take responsibility for my decisions and
their effect on me and others."

Planning, for some people, implies restraints. They
equate it with rigidity, being "locked in." People who
don't plan often regard themselves as free spirits; they're
turned off by any suggestion of following a prearranged
schedule. Of course, there's such a thing as overplanning
—attempting to control every detail and leaving no room
for spontaneity or the unexpected. But planning does not
have to be compulsive or inflexible. It should be a freeing

experience: instead of your being at the mercy of change or just an agent for the plans of others, you can gain control over how you spend your time, and shape your life according to your own needs and values.

All of us do a certain amount of planning, whether we realize it or not. If we didn't, our lives would be chaotic. Even people who say "I never plan" or "I hate to plan" would probably find, if they analyzed how they get through a day, that they're at least attempting to impose some sort of order on their activities.

Yet how many of us have confidence in our ability to make plans and carry them out successfully? When we see how often our "best-laid plans" don't work out, we may wonder whether there is any point in trying to arrange and organize when it would be so much simpler just to let things happen spontaneously. But when things don't work out as we'd like them to, it is usually not due to fate or unlucky circumstances but to some fault in the planning. Effective planning, like effective communication and problem-solving, is a *process* that takes several stages and involves thought, skill, and practice.

Hopefully, planning can give you an opportunity to expand and grow, to achieve the full and complete use of your potential. Psychologist Abraham Maslow called this ultimate form of personal fulfillment "self actualization," and found it in healthy, successful people who were able to meet most of their needs and at all levels.

MASLOW'S HIERARCHY OF NEEDS

Maslow found that people have five levels of needs; when they're deprived of needs satisfaction at any of them, their personal growth and development are limited. He placed the five levels in a hierarchy, ranging from the most basic to the more complex:

Level I: Physical Survival Needs

These are basic needs for such things as food, warmth, shelter—those that must be met for biological survival. When we are deprived of these needs, we are so driven to meet them that we have little interest in anything else.

Level II: Security Needs

When survival needs are taken care of, we become aware of the need to feel secure. We need to feel free from physical danger and psychological harassment, free to move about safely and express ourselves without fear of punishment or ridicule. When we live in fear, our energies are concentrated on protecting ourselves, and we can accomplish very little.

Level III: Social or Relationship Needs

We all need relationships with others. At this level, we need to feel we belong—to a family, group, community. We need intimacy, acceptance, understanding, and the ability to give and receive love. Deprived at this level, we often feel alienated, bored, joyless, disconnected, isolated.

Level IV: Achievement and Success Needs

Now another set of needs emerges—the need to be productive, creative, to have a feeling of accomplishment. These needs are important for our sense of self-worth; they're met when we set ourselves a goal and carry it out successfully. Deprived of these needs, we suffer a loss of self-esteem and develop insecure feelings about our ability to obtain satisfaction.

Level V: Self-actualization Needs

When people succeed in getting their needs met at Levels I–IV, they're motivated toward achieving self-actualization or self-fulfillment. According to Maslow, self-actualizing people are people whose life experiences have greater richness, heightened awareness of living, completeness, wholeness, overwhelming moments of joy, unity, and understanding. He calls these "peak experiences."

As a first step in setting goals, we suggest that you use this hierarchy as a way of identifying some of your important needs.

SHORT-TERM AND LONG-TERM GOALS

When you think about developing goals to meet your needs, it can be helpful to divide them into categories: short-term and long-term.

A short-term goal is anything that can be accomplished in 30 days or less, such as losing a few pounds, learning to drive a car, redecorating the living room, finding a part-time job. A long-term goal takes more than 30 days to accomplish—for example, getting a promotion at your job, getting a Master's degree, saving enough money to buy a new car, writing a book.

Short-term goals are, of course, easier to plan for and accomplish. You are more likely to stick to a 30-day than a 30-month diet. There is something discouraging about a goal that reaches so far into the future that you can hardly imagine reaching it. Therefore, long-term goals are made much more manageable by being broken down into a series of short-term goals so you can keep track of your progress along the way.

THE SIX-STEP PLANNING PROCESS

Planning for personal effectiveness follows the same six basic steps of the problem-solving process discussed in Chapter X.

Step I: Establishing Goals That Will Fulfill Your Needs or Wants

After you've carefully analyzed how you're using your time in relation to your present needs and wants, you can begin to establish some goals. This is easily the most important (and time-consuming) step of the planning process.

Make sure your goals accurately reflect your *present* needs. Past ways of spending your time may no longer be satisfying or fulfilling. They may even have become obsolete or unworkable. When situations in your life do change, either slightly (you receive a promotion) or drastically (you're a mother and a homemaker and your last child is preparing to leave home), you may need to make critical adjustments in your thinking and planning.

Make certain that your goals accurately reflect what *you* want to accomplish, not what you think you *should* want or what *someone else* wants for you. Many unhappy people work at jobs and engage in activities they dislike because they need to conform to societal expectations or because of the unsatisfied ambitions of another person, often a parent.

Women often choose roles and/or careers—wife, mother, nurse, teacher—mainly because women traditionally performed those jobs. And when people make mid-life career changes, one common reason is: "I've been following in my father's [or mother's] footsteps. Now I want to do something on my own."

Make sure your goals are realistic. Often, the difference

between satisfaction and dissatisfaction is in the individual's ability to set realistic goals. By "realistic" we mean goals that genuinely reflect inner needs and are within one's capabilities. It is not, for example, realistic to decide at the age of 35 that you'd like to become a concert pianist or a tournament tennis player. It might, however, be entirely realistic for you to decide at the same age that you'd like to return to college for an M.A. degree. A realistic goal takes into consideration personal limitations as well as aspirations.

In establishing goals for yourself, consider that, in general, long-term goals are more likely to satisfy needs at the upper levels. Effective social relationships and productive achievements usually require a substantial investment of time; most biological and security needs can be met in briefer periods. Also, short-term goals often deal with personal needs within our personal area of freedom and don't always require cooperation of others (which is usually necessary to meet most long-term goals).

To identify goals that meet your needs, we suggest you use Maslow's hierarchy. If some of your goals do not go beyond Levels I and II, if they do not offer an opportunity to grow toward self-actualization, they'll probably not bring you much in the way of personal fulfillment. Choosing mostly low-level goals may mean that you're underrating yourself or attempting to protect yourself against failure; you'd rather cut your aspirations way down to be sure of achieving them than risk falling short of a higher aim.

But unless you're willing to take some risk and reach out for what you really need and want, you'll never know the full range and extent of your potential. You will be denying yourself the opportunity for higher levels of achievement and satisfaction, for the experience of self-actualization.

Let's say that among the unfulfilled needs you identify

is this: you've been feeling bored, restless, vaguely dissatisfied. You feel a need for more mental stimulation, more intellectual development. We can use this unfulfilled need to go through the remaining steps of planning for personal effectiveness.

Step II: Collecting Ideas

This is the brainstorming stage, to help you develop the longest possible list of ideas, alternatives, and resources to help you achieve your goal. Be creative and imaginative. Do include ideas that seem "far out" at this point. Consult other people who might be able to help you. Draw on your own experience and on that of others who are willing to share their ideas and knowledge with you. Write down every idea that comes to mind or that is suggested by others.

To meet your need for increased mental stimulation, your list might include these alternatives:

Read more interesting books.

Take college courses.

Attend lectures, debates.

Invite interesting people to speak at your church or club.

Start independent study of a particular subject.

Organize a group of friends into a reading club to meet once a month.

Get information from others about what's exciting to them.

Watch interesting, controversial programs on television.

Join a particular organization—political, religious, etc.

Engage your family in interesting debates, discussions.

Form a group of coworkers to meet at lunchtime, after work, etc.

Subscribe to interesting magazines and journals.

Step III: Evaluating Ideas

When all the ideas have been collected and organized in some grouping, begin eliminating those that seem unworkable for one reason or another. Analyze, compare, contrast each of the remaining ideas until you're satisfied that one idea—or a combination of ideas—fits your situation.

Evaluate each alternative and come up with possible solutions. These include:

Take a college course (there is a college nearby where you can take courses through Adult Education at low cost).

Try to form a group of friends to meet monthly to discuss interesting topics.

Check out interesting books from the library.

During this stage, discuss your plans with your husband and children. Consider how they will be affected, what problems they might have with course scheduling, with group meetings in your home, etc.

Step IV: Planning to Take Action

At this stage you prepare to take action. Your decision includes plans to:

Enroll in one college course for the next semester

Call friends and acquaintances to try to generate a discussion group

Go to library twice a month to check out at least one interesting book

Step V: Taking Action

Now you'll be taking the necessary steps for carrying out your action plan. To get moving, you:

Check schedule, choose an interesting course, and enroll in school.

Start calling friends to interest them in discussion group, set date for first meeting.

Check out first book from the library.

Step VI: Evaluating Results

It's important to check your progress as you move toward your goal, to be sure you're carrying out each activity according to your original plan. Without such evaluation, you increase the risk of being sidetracked. Invariably you'll hit moments of discouragement on the way to a goal. Sometimes you'll be distracted from your plan. Complications and delays may be unavoidable—illness in the family or some personal problem that must take precedence over everything else. Or you may pick up information that causes you to reconsider one or more parts of the plan.

Evaluate your plan soon after you put it into action and at intervals later to make sure it's meeting your needs for increased mental stimulation. If not, consider other alternatives. You may find that the three activities you chose take more time than you planned to spend. You may decide to eliminate one.

In case of unavoidable delay, simply reschedule and continue as before. A good, carefully thought-through plan should have enough flexibility to accommodate necessary scheduling changes. The guiding principle is: keep to your original time schedule as closely as possible, but if achieving your goal is really important to you, don't abandon your plan because you need to rearrange your calendar.

The same principle applies if part of your plan proves unworkable. When this happens, some people lose faith in the entire plan and decide that the goal is simply not achievable. The trouble may merely be that the parts don't add up to the whole. One or more parts may need to be reworked. You may need to go back to one of the preceding steps.

Planning for personal effectiveness—like much else in E.T.W.—takes time, thought, patience, and persistence. But when you take responsibility for your life and, through your own assertive actions, achieve goals that fulfill your important needs, the rewards can be significant.

A CREDO
For Your Relationships with Others

When you're in control of your life, you can look back to the past or forward to the future and see yourself in a clear outline—because your life is your own creation, based on a firm sense and knowledge of yourself. As a general philosophy for your personal development and your relationships, we suggest the following Credo:

> You and I are in a relationship that is important to me, yet we are also two separate persons with our own individual values and needs.
>
> So that we will better know and understand what each of us values and needs, let us always be open and honest in our communication.
>
> Whenever I am prevented from meeting my needs by some action of yours, I will tell you honestly and without blame how I am affected, thus giving you the chance to modify your behavior out of respect for my needs. And I want you to be as open with me when my behavior is unacceptable to you.
>
> And when we experience conflicts in our relationship, let us agree to resolve each conflict without using

power to win at the expense of the other losing. We will always search for a solution that meets both of our needs—neither will lose, both will win.

Whenever you are experiencing a problem in your life, I will try to listen with acceptance and understanding in order to help you find your own solutions rather than imposing mine. And I want you to be a listener for me when I need to find solutions to my problems.

Because ours will be a relationship that allows both of us to become what we are capable of being, we will want to continue relating to each other—with mutual concern, caring, and respect.

APPENDIX: A BASIC RELAXATION EXERCISE

Here is an abbreviated procedure for practicing deep muscle relaxation and deep breathing. The eleven steps normally take about ten minutes.

You can sit in a chair or lie on the floor. At home, wear loose, comfortable clothing, remove your shoes, and choose an area free from major distractions. Do the exercises slowly. Let yourself experience the sensations. Learn how your body feels and how it behaves. After you've achieved some skill in relaxing your body, you may want to continue practicing in a less comfortable, private setting by simulating the setting in which you actually experience your anxiety (for example, do the exercises sitting or standing.)

You may also wish to get books, tapes or records, or a class that teaches these and more advanced skills.

1. *Prepare (1 minute).* Lie down on your back; relax your feet and hands; your palms should be up; your feet rolled apart slightly; let your head roll slightly to one side; sink into the floor; close your eyes; relax.

2. *Deep Breathe (2 minutes)*. Start your first deep breath by pushing your stomach out and filling it with air, then your chest, then your throat and nose; hold (about 5 seconds), then let the air out by drawing your stomach in first, then emptying your chest, throat, and nose; feel how relaxed you are; now start the second breath; breathe in slowly and deeply; exhale; now the third breath; notice how comfortable and relaxed you feel.

3. *Tense Toes (1 minute)*. Now curl your toes hard toward the floor; hold the tension (10 seconds); let go and relax; breathe slowly and deeply; now, fan the toes upward and out; hold tight (10 seconds); let go; relax; notice the comfortable, warm sensation in your feet.

4. *Tense Legs (30 seconds)*. Tense the muscles in both legs at once; hold (10 seconds); let go; relax your legs completely; let them sink into the floor; continue to breathe slowly and deeply (5 seconds).

5. *Tense Buttocks (30 seconds)*. Squeeze your buttocks together; hold (5 seconds); now let go; let your body sink into the floor; breathe slowly and relax.

6. *Tense Stomach (30 seconds)*. Tense your stomach; squeeze out the tension that may be there; hold tight (10 seconds); let go; feel a warm, relaxed sensation.

7. *Tense Arms and Shoulders (30 seconds)*. Shrug your shoulders up high and tighten your fists and arms; hold (10 seconds); let go of these muscles; sink back into the floor; relax and be comfortable.

8. *Tense Body (1 minute)*. Now, tense your entire body—every muscle; make a big frown on your face; hold (10 seconds); let go all at once; sink deeply into the floor; let everything go loose, limp, and relaxed; lie quietly for a moment.

9. *Focus on "Third Eye" (30 seconds)*. Now, let your head roll slightly to one side, relax your jaw; let your lips part; keep your eyes closed, and concentrate on the space between your eyes; let your eyes find and see that space—that "third eye"; focus on it; breathe slowly and deeply; relax; let all of your attention, thoughts, and feelings focus on your third eye; sink into that space; let it absorb your mind.

10. *Imagine Yourself in a Beautiful Place (2 minutes).* In your third eye, begin to see the most beautiful scene you've ever wanted to see; let the image form; take your time; let that place come into focus (10 seconds); now see yourself in that special place; be there; experience good feelings about being there; notice how relaxed and comfortable you are; stay in that beautiful place; breathe slowly and deeply as you have learned to do (60 seconds).

11. *Conclude (60 seconds).* Now, let the picture of your beautiful place slowly fade (15 seconds); open your eyes; slowly sit up and conclude the exercise.

A PERSONAL POSTSCRIPT

Being involved in studying women's issues, in designing the E.T.W. course, and in writing this book has been and continues to be a very exciting and stimulating experience for me. I find myself gradually changing in ways that I like—I am becoming less shy and more self-disclosing; gaining more confidence in myself; growing more aware of and sensitive to others; and becoming more accepting of my anger as I realize how valuable it is in motivating me to get the courage to say and do things about which I feel strongly.

And I am gratified and delighted to hear about other women's experiences; about how they are able to put this philosophy and these skills into practice in their own lives —at their own pace—in their own ways.

Since we started offering the E.T.W. course, in January, 1978, many women have sent in reports of how important this experience was for them. For some it was the first time they had taken a course for women and with other women. Others reported their new awareness of how completely involved in meeting the needs of others they had been and how much courage it took for them even to think about meeting some of their own needs. Some said they changed slightly; others said the changes were exciting, even dramatic.

Most reported that their husbands, children, friends, or coworkers responded positively to their increased self-disclosure and self-confidence, although some had the opposite experience: finding that some people with whom they had related before didn't like the changes they were making.

Many reported that this process wasn't easy, that they needed more practice and experience, and that they appreciated the modeling and coaching of the instructor and the support of other women in their class and of their families and friends.

Finally, while I don't like the idea of using "skills" to improve human relationships—skills seem mechanical and technical—we haven't found a better way to get such ideas across so people can use them in an everyday, practical way. And we do know that when people use these skills, they often make significant improvements in their personal lives and in their interpersonal relationships. It is my hope that they will seem like skills for the shortest possible time; that they will become so internalized that they no longer will be skills—they will be part of you.

Linda Adams
Leucadia, California
January, 1979

ACKNOWLEDGMENTS

I wish to acknowledge the contributions of the following people:

Elinor Lenz, who collaborated with me in the initial stages of writing this book.

My friend and colleague Kathleen Cornelius, who contributed to the initial development of the E.T.W. course and now so capably trains instructors to teach it.

Tony Zener, who made substantial contributions to the final version of the E.T.W. course.

The E.T.W. instructors—both women and men—who taught this course so successfully during its first year.

All those women who have taken the E.T.W. course— and have sent me some truly exciting reports of their experiences in applying what they learned to their own lives.

My coworker and friend Nancy Elkins, whose help was invaluable to me. I appreciate not only her typing the final draft of this manuscript, but her enthusiasm, her strength, and her honesty.

Nancy Montgomery White, Diane Kraus, Stephanie

Austin, and Stephanie Stratmann for their clerical assistance.

Peter Wyden, who contributed his editing expertise.

My husband, Tom Gordon, who edited some chapters of this book, but, more important, has contributed so much to my thinking about equitable relationships in the past ten years. I also appreciate his confidence in me and the continuing support he has given me.

My daughter, Michele, who contributes so much to my life with her honesty, her wit, her fairness, and her tolerance.

And all those people who had the courage and insight to write books about women that inspired and motivated me—Simone de Beauvoir, Kate Millett, Jean Baker Miller, Mary Daly, to name a few.

L.A.

SOURCES OF CHAPTER QUOTES

Chapter I	Babylonian Talmud.
Chapter II	La Fontaine, *Fables.*
Chapter III	Viola Spolin quoted in "Spolin Game Plan for Improvisational Theater" by Barry Hyams, *L.A. Times,* May 26, 1978.
Chapter IV	Martin Buber, *Between Man and Man.*
Chapter V	Sidney Jourard, *The Transparent Self.*
Chapter VI	Erasmus, *Adagia.*
Chapter VII	Joyce Brothers, "When Your Husband's Affection Cools," *Good Housekeeping,* May, 1972. Charlotte Painter, *Revelations: Diaries of Women,* with Mary Jane Moffat.
Chapter VIII	Rollo May, *The Meaning of Anxiety.*
Chapter IX	Jean Baker Miller, *Toward a New Psychology of Women.*
Chapter X	Thomas Gordon, *Parent Effectiveness Training.*

Chapter XI   Margaret Mead, *Sex and Temperament in Three Primitive Societies.*

Chapter XII   Seneca, *Ad Lucilium.*

Chapter XIII   Charleszetta Waddles quoted in "Mother Waddles: Black Angel of the Poor" by Lee Edson, *Reader's Digest,* October, 1972.

Chapter XIV   Patricia McLaughlin quoted in *American Scholar,* Autumn 1972.

BIBLIOGRAPHY

Alberti, Robert, and Michael Emmons. *Your Perfect Right.* San Luis Obispo, Cal.: Impact, 1970, 1974.

Gordon, Thomas. *Parent Effectiveness Training.* New York: Peter H. Wyden, Inc., 1970, 1975.

Johnson, Paula. "Women and Power: Toward a Theory of Effectiveness," *Journal of Social Issues.* Ann Arbor: The Society for the Psychological Study of Social Issues, 1976.

Jourard, Sidney M. *The Transparent Self.* New York: D. Van Nostrand Company, 1971.

May, Rollo. *The Meaning of Anxiety.* New York: W. W. Norton & Co., 1977.

Miller, Jean Baker. *Toward a New Psychology of Women.* Boston: Beacon Press, 1976.

SUGGESTED READING LIST

Books for Consciousness-raising

Beauvoir, Simone de. *The Second Sex.* New York: Alfred A. Knopf, 1952.

Gornick, Vivian, and Barbara Moran, eds. *Woman in Sexist Society.* New York: Basic Books, 1971.

Greer, Germaine. *The Female Eunuch.* New York: McGraw-Hill, 1971.

Horner, Matina. *The Feminine Personality in Conflict.* Belmont, Cal.: Brooks/Cole Publishing Company, 1971.

Kanter, Rosabeth Moss. *Men and Women of the Corporation.* New York: Basic Books, 1971.

Miller, Jean Baker. *Toward a New Psychology of Women.* Boston: Beacon Press, 1976.

Millett, Kate. *Sexual Politics.* Garden City, N.Y.: Doubleday & Co., 1970.

Morgan, Robin, ed. *Sisterhood Is Powerful.* New York: Random House, 1970.

Books on Assertiveness

Alberti, Robert, and Michael Emmons. *Your Perfect Right.* San Luis Obispo, Cal.: Impact, 1970, 1974.

Bloom, Lynn, et al. *The New Assertive Woman.* New York: Delacorte Press, 1975.

Bower, Sharon, and Gordon Bower. *Asserting Yourself.* Reading, Mass.: Addison-Wesley Publishing Co., 1976.

Button, Alan DeWill. *The Authentic Child.* New York: Random House, 1969.

Jourard, Sidney M. *The Transparent Self.* New York: D. Van Nostrand Company, 1964.

Lange, Arthur J., and Patricia Jakubowski. *Responsible Assertive Behavior.* Champaign, Ill.: Research Press, 1976.

Phelps, Stanlee, and Nancy Austin. *The Assertive Woman.* San Luis Obispo, Cal.: Impact, 1975.

Books on Values Clarification, Goal Setting, and Life Planning

Bowles, Richard. *What Color Is Your Parachute?* Berkeley: Ten Speed Press, 1972.

Hennig, Margaret, and Anne Jardim. *The Managerial Woman.* New York: Anchor Press/Doubleday, 1976.

Jongeward, Dorothy, and Dru Scott. *Women as Winners.* Reading, Mass.: Addison-Wesley Publishing Co., 1976.

Lenz, Elinor, and Marjorie H. Shaevitz. *So You Want to Go Back to School.* New York: McGraw-Hill, 1977.

Maslow, Abraham. *Toward a Psychology of Being.* New York: D. Van Nostrand Company, 1962.

Pogrebin, Letty Cottin. *Getting Yours.* New York: David McKay Co., 1975.

Sheehy, Gail. *Passages.* New York: E. P. Dutton & Co., 1976.

Simon, Sidney, et al. *Values Clarification.* New York: Hart Publishing Co., 1972.

FOR INFORMATION ABOUT
THE E.T.W. COURSE

If you are interested in enrolling in the E.T.W. course, write or phone

Effectiveness Training
E.T.W. Department
531 Stevens Avenue
Solana Beach, CA 92075
Phone: (714) 481-8121

Anyone who would like to be trained and authorized as an E.T.W. instructor and organizations interested in introducing the E.T.W. course for the development of their employees, supervisors, or executives, write or phone

Effectiveness Training
Instructor Training Department
531 Stevens Avenue
Solana Beach, CA 92075
Phone: (714) 481-8121

Index